KASPAR and the Iron Poodle

Andersen Young Readers' Library

J. K. Hooper

KASPAR and the Iron Poodle

Illustrated by Tony Ross

Andersen Press · London

For Nicholas Lake, who is too young to read this book,
Paul Devlin, who is a bit too old,
and Michael Moss, who is just right.

First published in 1982 by
Andersen Press Limited,
19-21 Conway Street,
London W.1.

British Library Cataloguing in Publication Data

Hooper, J.K.
Kaspar and the iron poodle.—(Andersen young readers' library)
I. Title
823'.914 [J] PZ7

ISBN 0-86264-034-2

Printed in Great Britain

1

'And now,' said Mrs Klotz, reaching up for the old biscuit tin beside the clock, 'I'm going to give you the money for the sausages. You won't forget them, will you?'

Her voice was anxious as usual, but more so, as money was important. (This was because they hadn't got much.) Kaspar was about to grumble, but Mrs Klotz rarely stopped speaking and she was off again.

'I'd go myself rather than trust you, but Mrs Smicksmack is planning to go to America next month to see some relations and I've promised to give her a hand this afternoon. She's getting her clothes ready to be packed. She has some lovely things. You should see them!'

She stood on tiptoe in front of the mirror to push a long pin through her little black hat. Catching a glimpse of herself in the skimpy frock and tight black coat, her face grew sadder. Her blue eyes were small and watery and her pinched nose was red at the end.

She always looks as though she's got a cold, thought Kaspar. He stared at her meagre back and skinny legs and ankles. They seemed thin enough to snap, although she couldn't weigh much. 'I'm usually finished by three, but I bet she keeps me another hour.'

Mrs Klotz, who helped to clean the grand apartment across the street was very proud of her imagined close relationship with her employer. Visions of Mrs Smicksmack's finery floated past her eyes. Her hands twitched as she thought of it.

'She's got real silk underwear, and satin dresses and fur wraps stuffed into every wardrobe. Much more than one woman could possibly need.'

Sometimes, when Mrs Smicksmack was out for the day, Mrs Klotz would set down her dustpan and sneak into Mrs Smicksmack's dressing room just to feel them. She would breathe in their expensive aroma as she ran her hands through the folds.

'There now,' she sniffed, patting the lapels of her coat and turning round to the table. 'That will have to do. Hold your hand out. I want to see that you get just the right amount.' Kaspar transferred the fork to his left hand and went on picking at the cold meats while his mother counted out the money.

'Mr Grinser is expecting you. I had a word with him just last night and I told him that you'd call in after school, so don't forget. And look after the money! Put it in the pocket with the button on it. There, do it now, or you're sure to leave it on the table.'

Kaspar was now obliged to put down the fork as his mother was dithering about him. Unwillingly he stuffed the coins into his leather trousers and pressed the pocket shut with a snap. Orders, orders, orders. Why was his mother always telling him to do things? But now she was going. At last he could finish his breakfast in peace.

'It's time I went. Mrs Smicksmack will be at the window. You know, she always looks to see what time I leave the house. She sees that she gets her money's-worth. Now don't sit there all day. Get a move on, or you'll be late! I'm sure that clock's slow.' She darted over to the mantelpiece, looked disbelievingly at the clock and slammed down the biscuit tin.

'Do you hear what I say? Drink your coffee. I'm off. Have you got your latchkey?'

She banged out of the living room and into the little passage that led to the door of the flat.

'Mr Grinser knows you're coming. Don't dawdle back from school! And be careful with the money!'

The flat door clicked and he heard her clattering off down the landing.

Kaspar sighed. Half an hour with his mother made him feel a hundred years older. He cut some ryebread with the big, steel knife and shoved it with the meat into his schoolbag. A strange smile stole into his eyes and he rummaged in the bag. He took out a matchbox and slid it open. It contained the corpse of a large black beetle. He closed it and put it into his pocket. Then he pulled a jumper on over his shirt, picked up his bag and left the flat.

The ramshackle house in which they lived was one of the last of its kind on the smart avenue. It was still surrounded by a high wall and one or two miserable trees. But the garden was a desolation of flattened earth and bits of junk. Eventually it would all be pulled down and new shops and flats would take its place.

Kaspar ran all the way downstairs then jumped the last six. The front door stood ajar and he dashed out into the sunlight and along the cracked concrete path. Mrs Krug's cat, Oscar, fled for safety – a white and orange streak heading for the wall.

Matty was waiting by the gate. He was dark, like an Italian, and played the accordion. He had one of his own. Kaspar wrenched the gate till the hinges creaked and let it bang on the wall behind him. At Mrs Smicksmack's kitchen window, Mrs Klotz winced. Kaspar and Matty strolled on in silence.

Johnnie and Christa joined them at the next corner. They too were members of Kaspar's gang. All four looked tired with black shadows under their eyes.

Christa yawned.

'What about tonight? We didn't take so much yesterday. I think people are getting tired of us.'

'Yes,' said Johnnie. 'Perhaps we should try somewhere else.'

Kaspar glanced at the other groups of schoolchildren that had begun the long march down the sunny avenue.

'Leave the thinking to me. The dock streets are the best sort of place. We won't be disturbed there by our parents. All we need is a new attraction.'

'What do you mean?' asked Matty.

'I've got an idea. Tell you about it tonight.'

They crossed the road at the traffic lights and headed down a narrow street of tall houses. Both sides were still shaded and it echoed with children's footsteps and voices. At the end of the street was the school.

Christa separated at the gate. The girls were taught

in a different part of the building.

'Usual time and place,' said Kaspar.

'I'll try. But they're getting suspicious at home. My mother doesn't go out at night like yours.'

Kaspar grinned wickedly. 'So what? It doesn't make any difference. She knows about me but I don't care. Last week she put a lock on my bedroom window. But I can pick locks!'

He disappeared with Matty and Johnnie into the mob in front of the boys' entrance. The crowd was beginning to sort itself out into a line. Old Schwanker, the caretaker, appeared in his grey uniform and walrus moustaches. Behind him, on the steps, came the Headmaster, Mr Pelikan, and two other teachers. Two only? thought Kaspar, and smiled one of his dark smiles.

There was his class-teacher, Mr Myrmidon, with lank black hair and a face like a griffon, and just in front of him, fat Miss Poltergeist, who was purple-cheeked and had hysterical pop-eyes. But no Miss Nesselfieber, hard and straight in her dishcloth cardigan and with a well-used ruler stuck beneath her arm.

Mr Pelikan began to bellow names from the register. Each boy shouted 'Present' then walked through the doorway while Mr Myrmidon, without looking up, ticked them off his list.

When it came to Kaspar's turn he made to enter the building but Mr Pelikan put a hand on his shoulder. The Headmaster's plump figure stiffened in his pale, perfectly-pressed suit and his pale eyes flickered behind rimless spectacles. Kaspar read the danger signals, but he was prepared. 'I wish to see you, Klotz. Be in my office in ten minutes.'

Inside, there was a brief announcement. Miss Nesselfieber had had a bicycle accident, fortunately not serious (here Kaspar received a flash from the spectacles) and would not be in school today. Her class would be divided between Miss Poltergeist and Mr Myrmidon. He, the Headmaster, would also take a small number personally for the last half-hour.

Before there was time for any reaction among the boys, Mr Myrmidon's voice ordered, 'To classes!' and they trooped off in silent, but joyous, lines. Miss Nesselfieber was not a favourite.

'Come in, come in!' snapped Pelikan. Kaspar stood to attention in front of the Headmaster's desk.

Pelikan sprang straight into the attack. 'The police officer who helped Miss Nesselfieber off the street this morning states that the bolt locking the handlebars on her bicycle was loose. Miss Nesselfieber, though in a state of shock, clearly remembers checking everything with her spanner only two days ago. I have no reason to doubt the accuracy of what she says. Have *you*, Klotz?'

'No, Mr Pelikan.'

'That is the first point. Here is the second. I see an entry in the Official Punishment Book, dated yesterday in which your name appears – "Repeatedly failing to do work at home, and impertinence – six strokes". Well?'

'Yes, Mr Pelikan.'

'What I wish to know is, is there the remotest possible

connection between these two events?'

'No, Mr Pelikan.'

Kaspar's face was blank. Pelikan's had grown pink.

'I see you do not bother to look surprised. At least you are a straightforward liar!'

Mr Pelikan's complexion deepened. His flabby hands began to twist his white handkerchief as though it were tightened round Kaspar's neck. 'My investigations will continue, Klotz. I am not content that it should remain a mystery. And the instant I can put my finger on some link with yourself, then you will hear from me again. You have been lucky in the past. But you must be made to realise that no one's luck can last forever.' (Kaspar was not sure about this. Perhaps he was the exception?)

The Headmaster, whose voice had been rising jerkily throughout his speech, paused to see if he were having any effect. Kaspar lowered his eyelids, just a fraction, not enough to be accused of insolence, but just enough to show boredom. 'Every time you see me,' Pelikan went on hotly, 'you will know that my mind is working on this issue. Your record in this school tells me that I need look no further for the author of this monstrous act. Your mother will be informed of my opinion,' Mr Pelikan ended weakly – he knew that this was not much of a threat. 'Now, return to your class, boy. Leave my sight!'

Leaving your sight is always a pleasure, thought Kaspar. A pretty ugly sight you are. But I will not return to my class. Not just yet.

When the door of the Headmaster's office closed behind him, he ignored Pelikan's instruction. Another way attracted him. The door to the staffroom stood open. He knew that at this hour it would be empty – especially, he thought pleasurably, as Miss Nesselfieber's absence was making extra work! His one concern was that Pelikan might emerge suddenly and catch him out. But at that moment the Headmaster's telephone bell rang and he knew that safety was guaranteed.

This would not take long. He glided across the room to Miss Poltergeist's locker and opened it. There was a mixed smell of strong cologne (Miss Poltergeist perspired heavily) and old dog. This latter evidently came from a travelling rug used by Miss Poltergeist's ancient dachshund, Max.

There it was – a generous object in green wickerwork, with dainty flowers woven into it. Miss Poltergeist's lunchbox! Kaspar had often seen it on the teacher's desk as he sat through midday detention classes. Miss Poltergeist would mark books and eat, occasionally flinging chalk at boys who tried to hold a conversation with each other. And for dessert (the part she liked best), she always brought a mouthwatering, giant cream cake. He picked the cake up and levered it apart with one finger. Then he reached into his pocket. A second later the dead black beetle was safely buried in a mountain of Mollendorf's finest cream. Kaspar patted the top of the cake into position, erased the fingermarks and admired the result. Not a trace of his attentions could be seen. With the care of an artist he replaced the confection exactly as it had been and returned the lunchbox to the locker.

There was a 'ching!' as the Headmaster hung up. Lesser boys might have panicked at this and dashed out, but not Kaspar. He waited silently to see what would happen next. Mr Pelikan began to set out fancy biscuits on a plate covered with a paper doily. It was almost time for his morning coffee.

When Pelikan did not come out of his office, Kaspar took a breath and walked quietly as a cat back to Mr Myrmidon's classroom.

It was lunch time. Kaspar sat alone by the boilerhouse while more energetic-seeming boys played football. The sky was high and blue. Matty and Johnnie sauntered up to him.

'Sit there, and be quiet,' said Kaspar. Their eyes followed his to the open window of the staffroom.

They saw Mr Myrmidon enter and cross to his locker. Kaspar did not stir. Then they saw Miss Poltergeist coming in, talking in her shrill voice. She hurried to the far end of the room and busied herself out of sight. A smile came to Kaspar's lips. Matty and Johnnie looked at each other wondering what was up.

Five minutes later – for Miss Poltergeist ate lovingly but not lingeringly – there came an explosive spitting noise, followed by a scream. The fat figure of Miss Poltergeist rocketed back across the window and disappeared into the washroom. The football game stopped and everyone in the playground stared. Ghastly sounds of vomiting proceeded from the washroom, till at last, after an interval of loud panting, the lavatory was flushed.

Kaspar laid both hands on his bare knees and smiled. The day had begun well.

2

'Yes. Yes. See you!' yelled Kaspar.

He was in a hurry to put his plan into effect. Old men and women stood and looked after him as he marched down the street. They waited for him to say, 'Nice day' or 'Good afternoon' – he was, after all, a neighbour's child – but he ignored them. He always did. They looked at each other and said, 'He's a bad one, that Kaspar Klotz.'

Mr Grinser's butcher's shop was shining and white. Sprigs of emerald parsley were placed about the clean trays where the meat was kept. Mr Grinser put down fresh sawdust every day and swept the shop out. But if you looked carefully you could see the big block and choppers in the back. They were often dripping with blood.

At the centre of the window was a plaster pig's head on a plate. The pig had wide, blue eyes with golden lashes and fat, pink cheeks. It always reminded Kaspar of Miss Poltergeist, except that the pig smiled and Miss Poltergeist never did. No matter whether the wind blew, or freezing rain spattered down the glass, the pig looked warm and radiant, and laughed at everyone. Mr Grinser thought it very beautiful and decorated it with paper roses. It was his household god.

Kaspar entered the shop.

'Ah, it's you, Kaspar!' said Mr Grinser, spreading his hands to hide the blood-smears on his white apron (he had blood beneath his fingernails too). 'Your mother told me to expect you. I hear she's extra busy today, eh?'

Mr Grinser liked to keep on good terms with Kaspar's mother, so he smiled at Kaspar from under his silly straw hat. But Kaspar was not fooled. He knew that Mr Grinser's first name was Adolphus and that he didn't like him one bit. 'She's helping Mrs Smicksmack,' was all that Grinser could get out of him.

'Well, well,' he said. And then, as Kaspar still stood dumbly, 'Well, well, well.'

The next one to speak is the loser, thought Kaspar. It won't be me.

'Well, I'll just go and get you those sausages, then.' Grinser turned to go into the back shop.

This was the moment Kaspar had been waiting for. His whole body tingled with excitement. But suddenly Grinser stopped. 'They're very nice today, if I say so myself.' Kaspar cursed him silently.

'Bit of extra spice! Your mother likes that, eh?' He winked. Kaspar didn't move a muscle. He could have won a staring match with the sphinx. 'Right-o,' sighed Mr Grinser, and went to get the parcel.

In a flash, Kaspar had the pig's head out of the window and stowed into his bag. He did up the buckle and turned round just as Mr Grinser re-appeared. He carried the sausages on a tissue and put a newspaper around them. Kaspar fumbled for the coins in his pocket, trying with one hand to keep his bulky schoolbag out of sight.

Mr Grinser watched him for a bit. Then his smile widened until Kaspar could see all his teeth, including the three gold fillings in his top set.

'Oh, that doesn't matter, lad! Tell your mother she can pay me next time I see her. She's a special customer. Now you hurry off and cook these for her tea. She'll be ready for 'em!' Kaspar grabbed the packet and manoeuvred himself to the door.

'Tell her from me they'll do her a bit o' good. 'Bye, 'bye, lad.'

The bell rang over the shop door and he was out!

'Ungrateful beggar,' grumbled Mr Grinser. 'Thank God he's not mine. I'd soon teach him a few manners.'

Out on the street, Kaspar thought, I will not run. That might look suspicious. But he did walk fast.

'A scarf with a hole in it!' wailed Mrs Klotz. 'I give up an hour and a half of my own precious time and *that's* what she calls a reward! With all *she's* got! Oh, she says, it's such a pretty thing, she says, and it's only a little cigarette burn and I'm sure it'll look lovely on you, Mrs Klotz. Not good enough for *her* though. High and mightiness!'

Kaspar's mind was elsewhere. He had other things to think about. Besides, his mother's relations with Mrs Smicksmack were always up and down. It wasn't worth the effort to follow them.

'I've a good mind to hand in my notice. She pays me fairly – and regularly – I'll grant you that. But when it comes to other things. Mean!'

'There's Mrs Krug. She was telling me just the other day about Mrs Krollenhof. *She* had a French maid – before she died, of course – and she wasn't half as rich as Smicksmack. But she left *her* cleaning lady an astrakhan fur coat in her will. It was a fairly old one, Krug says, but still good. That's a *lady* for you. But Smicksmack! Wealth's come to her too sudden. She's not used to it. You can see that. She keeps a tight fist. Why aren't you eating your sausages? They're good.'

'I was listening to you,' lied Kaspar.

'That makes a change. You're not like most boys – glad to have a chat with their mothers. You never talk to me. Well, go on, eat them up. Folks like us can't afford to waste good food.'

She spread out the silk scarf again to have a look at it. There was a tiny, brown-edged hole near one corner.

Apart from that, thought Kaspar, it was very beautiful. It was coloured dark grey and had twisting patterns of green and blue. When his mother handled it, it gleamed.

'Well, thanks very much for nothing, that's what I say,' said Mrs Klotz. She crumpled it into a ball and threw it onto the sideboard. 'Got better things myself.' Then her voice softened. 'Mr Grinser – he's a real friend. Wasn't it kind of him to give us those sausages, Kaspar?'

Kaspar grew wary.

'He said you had to pay for them next time you saw him.'

'Yes,' she went on, 'but he didn't mean it. I'll bet he refuses to take the money. He's a kind man, Mr Grinser.'

'I think you ought to pay him.'

'What for?' Mrs Klotz was indignant.

'I don't see why we have to depend on him!'

'You're a wicked boy, Kaspar, to talk of Mr Grinser like that. We need all the help we're given. I hope you remember that. Mr Grinser's been very good to me.' She looked at him defiantly, ready to pick a quarrel. 'I like him a lot.'

'I don't,' said Kaspar, half to himself.

'What's that you say?'

A spot of red appeared beside his mother's adam's apple. This was always a sign that she was about to fly into a temper. Kaspar thought of it as one petal of a whole, angry, red flower bursting up inside her. There was no point in arguing with her when she was in one of these moods. Kaspar pushed back his chair and stood up.

'What did you say, I said,' repeated Mrs Klotz, determined to pin Kaspar down if she could. He went to the door. 'And where do you think you're going now? In some houses children have to ask permission before they leave the table. But not in this one. Oh, no! You just please yourself!'

She began a description of Kaspar's failings, which he knew from experience would last at least a quarter of an hour. Luckily he had discovered several years earlier that his mother continued this oration whether he was present to hear it or not. He usually vanished at the outset.

No doubt she really wanted to go on about Grinser. Kaspar had a nasty feeling that those two were cooking something up together. But he refused to let her talk to him about it. He did not want to listen. Anyway, it was easy to get his mother's mind off the subject. She never thought about anything for long. She's not like me, he considered, I make plans, and I carry them out.

Mrs Klotz completed her review of Kaspar's deficiencies and ended in her usual manner. She promised herself for the hundredth time that somehow she would get on top of that boy. With or without Grinser, he must be brought to heel.

Later that evening Mr Grinser stepped out into the street and set off jauntily in the direction of the Green

Monkey. He had swapped his straw boater for a more impressive bowler hat, and his hand rested lightly on a slim, malacca cane.

By day he was content to seem a diligent and respectful shopkeeper; but when his shutters were closed he was his own man, and a smart one at that. The Green Monkey was his favourite pub, not only because he was a known and highly-valued customer there, but also because on most nights he was sure to catch a glimpse of Mrs Klotz over the glass screen of the Ladies' Parlour, as she sat sipping a port and lemon with her old friend, Krug.

She was certainly a pleasant-looking woman, Mrs Klotz, and Grinser complimented himself that she had the good taste to recognise his own charms. Sometimes he would buy a drink and send it in for her, and the thought of her grateful expressions brought a self-satisfied smile to his face.

He twiddled the small carnation he had stuck in his buttonhole, then fingered the heavy gold links of his watch chain. Yes, Mrs Klotz had the sense to see that he would make a fine match. If only there wasn't Kaspar to think about! Wasn't it just after Kaspar had called for the sausages this afternoon that he had first noticed the disappearance of his beautiful pig's head? He wouldn't put it past that kid to have pinched it when he wasn't looking. But what would a boy want with a pig's head made of plaster? On the other hand, what would *anyone* want with it? He would have to watch Kaspar. Especially as he had other things on his mind besides matrimony.

Still contemplating the pig mystery, Mr Grinser pushed open the swing door of the saloon bar. He went to the bar and ordered some pickled herring and a glass of gin.

'I've tried locking him in, Mrs Krug, and I always take his latchkey away from him at night, but he still gets out. I know he does.'

'A good hiding is what he needs, dear. What you should have is a man about the place as could do it for you.'

'Perhaps you're right, Mrs Krug.'

Mrs Klotz put on her coy expression. 'Do you think this brooch goes all right with my coat?'

'Looks a treat, dear. Are you ready now?' Mrs Krug didn't like wasting time once the pubs were open.

'Yes, just coming. But you're sure this brooch isn't a bit flashy?'

''Course not. I likes a bit o' sparkle meself. Come on, or our table'll be took. Some folks have no respect for regulars.'

'Right you are.'

They shuffled off, arm in arm.

Kaspar listened through his bedroom door until he heard the latch click. Then he pulled off the striped pyjamas he was wearing and hurried into his daytime clothes.

3

That was it! The lock on his window was open. Easy, thought Kaspar, as he shoved a penknife back into his pocket. He picked up an old suitcase and, leaning out, dropped it into the garden below. It was light and didn't make much noise.

Outside, the long summer dusk continued and people had put their lights on without bothering to close the curtains. This made things risky as he might easily be spotted. He scanned the buildings opposite for anyone standing at a window to watch the passing traffic. Then he followed his usual route along the drainpipe until he reached the ground.

He hurried to get off the Avenue with its busy shops and cafés and soon he was heading down a little side street, dark with trees. At the bottom was a line of railings and behind them the shrubbery of a small park. The gate was locked to keep out tramps at night, but the railings were widely-spaced and he got through them without difficulty. He pushed the suitcase through in front of him.

He advanced cautiously through the dusty bushes, stopped and whistled. Instead of someone whistling back there was a short silence. Then he heard two notes played on an accordion and there was silence again. It must be Matty.

He came to the edge of the bushes and peered out. Before him lay a tiny, browned lawn with the park

shelter on its far side. This was their headquarters.

'Been here long?'

'No, just got here before you. What about Johnnie and Christa?'

'They'll come.'

Kaspar was always sure of himself.

'Meanwhile, I want you to find me a pole. A stick about your height would do.'

'What for?' Matty looked puzzled.

'I'll show you in a minute.'

'There are some gardeners' tools round at the back. They must have been tidying up today.'

'Fetch them.'

From the bundle of implements Kaspar selected a dutch hoe and a trowel with a longish handle.

'These'll do. Put the rest back.'

Johnnie and Christa arrived from the opposite

direction just as he was taking some cord from the suitcase. Johnnie carried a wooden crutch and a tin can. Christa wore a long skirt that reached to her ankles.

'Here,' said Kaspar, still crouching down. 'You can wear this tonight.'

He handed the silk scarf to Christa and she held it up to look at it. 'It's gorgeous,' she breathed. 'Where did you get it?'

'It's an old one of Smicksmack's. Put it on.'

She draped it around her shoulders and knotted it at the front. Then she skipped about over the lawn, making her skirt flare out. Moonlight rippled over the scarf.

'Not bad. Here, Matty, give me a hand. Hold the trowel like this.'

Kaspar lashed the cord around it, fixing the trowel to the hoe. It made a cross. 'This,' he said, 'is going to be our new attraction.'

The sickle moon had been joined by a few stars. Below them one or two seagulls wheeled in huge circles. Now the great birds could see the ships' lights reflected in the water. Now they were over the dark streets and black alleyways where tomcats hunted on the backyard walls. The harbour area smelt of diesel, salted fish and the sea.

From a pub called 'The Sailor's Farewell' a strong light streamed out onto the pavement. Two old men sat on wooden chairs, hanging on to mugs of beer. Men and women stood around expectantly and the heads of more bobbed up at the window. They were smiling and nudging each other.

Matty played a swelling arpeggio on his accordion. Kaspar stepped forward.

'Ladies and gentlemen. For your entertainment: the Street Theatre of Koningshaven!'

Immediately, Matty went into a fast tune that set their feet tapping. He played like a professional, swirling his instrument about. His dark eyes were happy or sad with the music. Johnnie, who had suddenly developed a limp, grabbed the tin can and hobbled around on his crutch. But it was too soon and the audience wanted more before it would pay.

Matty finished his first tune with a flourish, and there were murmurs of appreciation, but not much money yet. Then Christa jumped into the yellow light and danced in her swirling skirt. Several people began to hum and clap their hands to the well-known tune. It was called 'The Wandering Bird' and Christa always danced to it. One of the old seamen knew the words and joined in, in a bass voice. Now they were warming up! The tinkle of coins could be heard in the background as Johnnie did his stuff.

Kaspar was next with a display of acrobatics. He wasn't much of an acrobat but he could do a few cartwheels and walk on his hands. Anyway it gave Matty a well-needed break. There was less hand-clapping when he finished and one or two people moved to go inside. But now it was time for the 'new attraction'. Matty played a loud chord and up from behind the lamp-post sprang Christa holding a 'partner' at arm's length. The sight of the partner brought a chorus of cheers from the onlookers. There, mounted on the stick, with old gloves for hands and dressed in Mrs Klotz's most ancient winter coat, was the smiling face of Mr Grinser's pig!

Christa pretended to curtsy to it and then set off in a wild polka. The audience shouted in delight and encouraged her. Then Kaspar jumped out and after standing with his hands on his hips, looking jealous, whisked the pig away from her and danced it to a different tune. Christa stamped her foot, grabbed it back, and the two fought over it like this until the paper roses hung crookedly over its eyes. The old men were almost choking with laughter and managed to spill half of their beer over the flagstones, while the other spectators leaned against each other helplessly. Johnnie busied himself with the tin and it was good and heavy, when he brought it back this time!

Christa, Kaspar and the pig made a final bow (not too low in case the pig's head came off) and then they all stood together to say farewell. This was Johnnie's big moment. He had beautiful green eyes and he knew just how to use them. He came to the centre of the group and placed the tin at his feet. Then, leaning on his crutch, he looked up at the stars so that his eyes twinkled like them, and he began to sing a sad, old song about a little boy whose father had never come home to him. The accordion played softly in the background

and a sailor swayed gently with his girlfriend. Kaspar, feeling the solemnity of the moment, leant the pig against his shoulder and waltzed it slowly and mournfully across the street. Some of the women were dabbing at their faces with handkerchiefs and, as the tears began to flow, so did the cash. Rejoicing, the children swept up their takings and waved goodbye to their sentimental audience. Then they hurried off to find another pub.

It was eleven o'clock and in the saloon bar of the Green Monkey Mr Grinser was feeling on top form. He had spent a thoroughly enjoyable evening. The Green Monkey regulars had been treated to his opinions on a variety of important topics and he knew that his loud voice could easily be heard on the other side of the glass screen. He raised a friendly hand and waggled his fingers at Mrs Klotz to ask if she were ready for another port and lemon. But Mrs Klotz had picked up her handbag and was ready to leave.

'Just one more, dear,' pleaded Mrs Krug, who enjoyed her drink even more when someone else was paying for it. 'Seems a pity to disappoint the gentleman.'

'Yes, I know, Mrs Krug, but I daren't stay. I'm up early in the morning as you know and I'm feeling a bit tiddly already!'

She stood up and shook her head at Grinser, at the same time giving him a winning smile. He raised his eyebrows in a look of mock pleading but she only shook her head again and began buttoning up her coat. Krug drained her glass and banged it down on the table. Her old joints creaked as she struggled up from the bench.

'Some folks don't know when they're well off,' she muttered. 'It's a lot cosier here than back at that house.'

At the door, Grinser was waiting for them. 'Would you two ladies do me the honour of allowing me to escort you home?'

Krug sniffed at the aroma of hair cream, gin and pickled herrings, but she smiled alluringly at him and Mrs Klotz coloured up with pleasure. Grinser gave an arm to each and they giggled when he dropped his cane.

'You should have been an octopus, Mr Grinser,' said Mrs Krug.

'Really, Mrs Krug? Now what do you think I'd get up to with all those extra arms!'

He winked at them both, which set them off giggling again, and they moved a little unsteadily up the street.

'Not a bad sort, Grinser,' said Mrs Krug to Kaspar's mother when he had left them at the gate. 'You could do worse.'

Mrs Klotz feigned surprise. 'Oh, Mrs Krug. I don't know what you mean. What on earth would Mr Grinser see in me?'

Mrs Klotz was hoping that Mrs Krug would think of something nice to say about her, but at that moment Old Krug remembered the drink she had turned down and stopped feeling complimentary.

'Beats me, dear. They're funny creatures, men.'

Krug left her, feeling slightly disappointed, at the first landing. 'Bet that boy of yours 'as been up to mischief again. Ten to one he's not in bed where 'e should be. Pity he's not the kind of boy Grinser could take a liking to. Sweet dreams, dear.'

'Goodnight!'

Mrs Klotz stamped up the last flight. Sometimes she didn't know why she bothered with Old Krug.

In the flat she switched on the light and hurried to Kaspar's bedroom. She was right, the old sourpuss. He was nowhere to be seen. She thought of Mr Grinser's kind smile. And then she thought of Kaspar. Kaspar's reign would have to come to an end. She'd think of something to cure him – just see if she didn't.

Police Constable Hammelpranger came to a wheezing halt in the middle of the road. His lungs were long past the strain of running and now his legs had packed in too. He glowered at the backs of the escaping children as they disappeared round yet another corner and fanned his hot face with his cape.

He had come across them acting in front of the Duck and Jellyfish and had chased them as far as here. Well, at least they were off *his* patch. He ran a large forefinger round the inside of his collar and glared at the grinning passers-by. He tried to resume his way with dignity but every now and then he gave a wheeze, which he tried to pretend was a cough.

'Where to now?' panted Johnnie.

Anyone who had seen him previously that evening would have been amazed at the nimbleness with which the little lame boy had shouldered his crutch and pelted down the street.

'Let's make for the river,' said Kaspar. 'Is the money O.K.?'

'You bet,' said Johnnie. 'That's the last thing I would let go of.'

Later, they huddled together on one of the benches under the sweet-smelling lime trees and counted their takings. A light mist rolled towards them off the water.

'Not bad, not bad,' murmured Kaspar. 'What say you we spend some of it now?'

'Agreed!' shouted the others.

'Right. You two stay here and Matty can help me do the carrying.'

Matty laid his accordion down on the gravel and accompanied Kaspar to Coffee Nickel's. This was a little stall set up by the river. It was lit by a bright storm lantern. From it, delicious smells of hot food and good coffee wafted to their nostrils. Coffee Nickel was the small dumpy man in a white overall who kept the stall. He always had the stump of a black cigar stuck in the corner of his mouth so that he had to talk out of the other side. His voice was gruff but he was always in a good humour.

'Evening, gents. Do you want the usual?'

Kaspar and Matty nodded. They watched him hungrily as he sliced up the long rolls. Then he took a pair of tongs and filled them with steaming frankfurters from the vat.

'Mustard on one and the others plain. That's right, isn't it?'

Kaspar and Matty nodded again. They were pleased at the idea of being well-known customers. Kaspar paid and began to carry them back while Matty held the four paper cups of sweet coffee.

They were walking quickly because their hands were burning, and were halfway back to the bench, when three tall boys stepped out from under the lime trees.

Before they could do anything about it, they found themselves pinioned by two of the boys while the leader rifled their pockets. He found the remaining cash on Kaspar, counted it quickly and stood back, smiling.

'That's a fair-sized haul for a couple of hours' work. You're quite a little goldmine, aren't you?'

Kaspar wriggled to get free, but he was hampered by the hot buns.

'You give that back! And let us go or I'll report you to the police!'

The leader laughed.

'The police would be very glad to meet you again, but I think you'll find us much more friendly. Isn't that right, lads?'

The other two laughed with him and shook Kaspar and Matty just to show how friendly they were. 'Get off!' yelled Matty. 'You're spilling our coffee!'

'Dear, dear, what a shame. You'd better be gentle with him, Ernst, or he'll get hot coffee all down his little white shirt front. Yes, that's Ernst by the way and the other bloke's Ferdy. My name's Rudolf and we've been dying to make your acquaintances for ages.'

Kaspar stared at him. 'What do you want from us?' he growled, eyeing the money in Rudolf's paw.

'Oh, that's easy. Just stuff like this - and more like it.' His face hardened. 'This is *our* area, Mr Entertainer, and whatever you pick up here, we'll have a share of. See? Now then,' his lips curled into a smile again, 'you'll not find us greedy. We don't want to kill the goose that lays the golden eggs. Just see that you keep on laying, that's all.'

Now that Kaspar understood the situation his defiance returned. 'What if we don't pay up?'

Rudolf's smile didn't change. 'That wouldn't be very intelligent. You're not a blockhead, are you? We could tip off the police about where to expect you and that wouldn't be good for business would it? Also, there's Ferdy and Ernst here. They're very muscular boys as you can see and they like a bit of exercise, don't you, lads?'

Ernst and Ferdy grinned.

'They'd be very annoyed if they didn't get their pocket money. So, all in all, I think it's a good idea if we become business partners. What about you?'

Thinking it the quickest way out of the mess, Kaspar agreed. He was sure they would be able to avoid this mob once they got away.

'Excellent!' said Rudolf. 'You're a very wise boy. Now, what do you call yourself?'

'Kaspar, Kaspar Klotz.'

As soon as he'd given his name away, he wished he hadn't.

'Klotz?'

The red-haired boy, Ferdy, had a soft voice.

'His mother works for Mrs Smicksmack on the Schiller Avenue.'

Rudolf gave him a sharp look and then gazed at Kaspar.

'That right?'

'Yes.'

'Good. I can see you're going to be a useful type to know. Right! Let's go, lads. We've detained our new friends long enough. Here you are, Mr Kaspar Klotz, just to show we've got your best interests at heart.'

To Kaspar's surprise, Rudolf dropped about half of the coins back into his pocket.

'See you around then.'

'We – we don't come here every night,' said Kaspar.

'Oh, don't worry about that,' grinned Rudolf. 'We do.'

4

Supported by cushions of apricot silk, the still-beautiful Smicksmack lay on her morning divan grunting delicately as she crouched over one foot. Her satiny dressing gown hung about her in folds and her little pink tongue flickered playfully in and out as she finished painting her toenails an emerald green to match her eyes.

She completed her toilette, screwed the tiny brush back into its bottle and straightened herself up with a grunt slightly less delicate than the ones before.

'Coffee ready, Mrs Klotz?' she enquired, in a clear, bell-like soprano.

'Just coming, Mrs Smicksmack,' said a voice. 'Would you care for biscuits?'

The little pink tongue did a fandango over the teeth again, this time exploratively. Mrs Smicksmack was thinking of the charming new dentist and his advice about fillings.

'Biscuits? No, not for *me* this morning. But *do* bring them in if you would like a nibble yourself!'

She waved her slender legs about to complete the drying of the nail varnish. Then she made herself more comfortable in the cushions and had composed a bright, welcoming smile on her face just as Mrs Klotz entered with the tray.

'There now, Mrs Klotz. What *would* I do without you?' Her pencilled eyebrows lifted. 'Ah, I see you've brought *two* cups!'

Why she always seemed surprised about this, Mrs Klotz never knew. This was obviously one of the best parts of Mrs Smicksmack's day. She would lie on the sofa for at least half an hour – no doubt recovering from the shock of getting out of bed – sipping coffee from a white, porcelain cup, and pumping Mrs Klotz gently for all the gossip. Mrs Klotz had long ago formed the habit of taking coffee with her rather than fiddling about aimlessly with her duster.

'Now, bring over a chair, dear, and tell me all the *news*.'

Mrs Klotz always racked her brains to find something interesting. She much preferred chatting with Mrs Smicksmack to heaving about the heavy vacuum cleaner or stuffing Mrs Smicksmack's dirty linen into the laundry basket, or even dusting the thousand and one precious objects about the rooms – though they were very pretty, she'd grant you that. But this morning she had only one thing on her mind and after detailing the latest developments in her romance with Mr Grinser (a subject that fascinated Mrs Smicksmack) she took up her old tale of woe about the disobedient Kaspar. 'I've done all I can with him, that I have, Mrs Smicksmack. I've cared for that boy, worked and scrubbed for him ever since he was a baby. How I've kept my temper at times I don't know!'

'Everyone knows you, Mrs Klotz. You have the patience of a saint.'

Mrs Smicksmack lowered her eyes sympathetically,

hoping that Mrs Klotz would take the hint and leave this boring subject. She expected something a little juicier from their morning get-together.

Unfortunately, Mrs Klotz, who wouldn't know a hint from a horsebox, merely resumed the same topic until Mrs Smicksmack was almost reduced to a state of coma. She attempted to combat this by thinking of all sorts of gay and amusing things like what she would eat for lunch and where they would go on the American trip but nothing seemed to help. She was going under for the third time when, unexpectedly, her brain came to her rescue.

'Mrs Klotz!' she announced (a little louder than was really necessary).

'Mrs Klotz!!'

'Yes, Mrs Smicksmack?'

'Have you ever heard me speak of our old and respected acquaintance, Mr Nebula?'

Mrs Klotz thought for a bit, then admitted that she couldn't say as she had. 'Why do you ask, Mrs Smicksmack? Do you think that Mr Nebula could . . . ?'

'Not Mr Nebula, Mrs Klotz – his dog!'

Mrs Smicksmack was so excited by her brainwave that she sprang up from the sofa in one bound and was halfway across the room before she remembered that she paid Mrs Klotz to fetch and carry for her.

'The evening paper, bring it here at once!'

'What, last night's paper? I'll see if I can find it. I think the cat was lying on it when I came in this morning.'

'Hurry, Mrs Klotz. There is no time to lose. Oh! How clever of me to think of it! If I am not mistaken, Mrs Klotz, Mr Nebula's poodle can solve all your problems before the week is out!'

Kaspar, Matty and Johnnie sat together in a corner of the boys' playground in an atmosphere of gloom.

'No,' Kaspar was saying. 'There's no point in starting work again until we've made a new plan. Rudolf's gang obviously know all our movements – and there's still old Hammelpranger to think about.'

'Why don't we concentrate on the Station Square for a bit?' suggested Johnnie. 'There are plenty of cafés there, and plenty of escape routes if we need them.'

Kaspar looked unimpressed. 'I've thought of that,' he said, 'but we're not going to be beaten on our own ground. We've got just as much right to be there as big Rudolf. Besides, there are dozens more pubs in the dockland. If we organize it carefully and don't stay too long in one place, I'm sure we can avoid them. They can't be *everywhere*.'

'But what are we actually going to do?'

'We're going to meet again tonight. They don't seem to know about the park hut, so we're still safe there. And one of you must bring a street map. You can get one from the public library. We'll work out a new plan from that.'

'I shan't need to bring my accordion then?'

'Not tonight, Matty. We've got to do some serious thinking. Now, split up. Nesselfieber's got her eye on us from the window. We'd better keep out of her way today. See you later.'

'Look, look, look. Here it is, Mrs Klotz.'

Mrs Smicksmack drew a large, red ring around a paragraph in the advertisements column.

'Now, just read that, won't you, and see if I'm not right!' She tapped excitedly at the end of her nose with her little gold pencil, until she saw that specks of face powder were being dislodged, so she tucked it back into her bag.

Mrs Klotz took the newspaper from her and screwed up her eyes. Her lips began to move soundlessly.

'Oh, read it *aloud*, Mrs Klotz, read it *aloud*!'

'Yes, Mrs Smicksmack. If you say so. It says here . . . .'

'Yes, yes?'

'Attractive budgie cage with stand. Owner emigrating. Also several saucepans.'

'What?'

Mrs Smicksmack's face purpled with impatience. 'No, not *that*! Oh, give it to me, Mrs Klotz. You are *hopeless* sometimes. Now, listen to me!'

Mrs Klotz tried to appear interested and intelligent as Mrs Smicksmack went on, 'All family and personal problems sorted out discreetly, by well-qualified and experienced poodle. Apply: Nebula, 97b Prince's Street.' There now, Mrs Klotz, get your hat and coat. You must go immediately, before he takes another case!'

'But the housework, Mrs Smicksmack - I haven't even started on the beds yet!'

'Leave the housework, leave the beds - just leave everything as it is, Mrs Klotz. You can always come back later. It is urgent that you get to Mr Nebula's as soon as possible. Off you go. I will ring Mr Nebula personally and tell him to expect you!'

'Oh, Mrs Smicksmack, I don't know what to say. It's so kind of you to take an interest in my little affairs.'

'Not at all, Mrs Klotz. As my employee you are entitled to my consideration. Besides, I can always deduct the cost of the telephone call from your week's wages. Now, go, Mrs Klotz, go quickly. The end of your problems is nigh!'

Mrs Klotz hurried down the Schiller Avenue in her tight-fitting black coat. She was not used to rapid decision-making and that (and Mrs Smicksmack's enthusiasm) had left her totally confused. It was only when she entered the impressive hallway of 97 Prince's Street and found the right door that her mind pondered for a moment on one word she remembered from the advertisement. The word was 'poodle'.

The door swung open and she found herself looking at a tall, elderly gentleman, dressed in a tailcoat.

'Mrs Klotz?'

'Yes,' she squeaked.

'Pray, come in. I have just this instant received a telephone message from my friend Mrs Smicksmack.

She has told me *all*.'

He wafted her into the apartment with a grave bow and preceded her into a large, but gloomy, study. A black marble clock ticked solemnly on the mantelshelf before a huge mirror, and Mrs Klotz could have sworn she noticed a small, varnished alligator hanging in the window before she was shown to a chair. She didn't like stuffed animals and she hoped it might be a trick of the light. Mr Nebula seated himself behind a gigantic desk and smiled patiently, waiting for her to speak.

'It's very good of you to see me at such short notice, Mr....' Mrs Klotz struggled to remember his name. Memory was not her strong suit.

'Nebula,' said the old gentleman. 'Olaf, Patrick, François, Igor, Pietro Nebula. As a matter of fact,' he added, 'I have many other Christian names!'

Mrs Klotz smiled weakly.

'My dear parents, you see, Mrs Klotz, intended that I should feel at home in whatsoever country I finally settled down. Consequently, they selected a name from all the major European languages and, of course, Chinese, Japanese and Hindi. They were an extremely thoughtful pair and I have much to be thankful for in my parentage. Indeed, it is partly as a tribute to their sacred memory that I go about offering my humble services to those in need. Would you kindly approach the desk and remove your hat?'

Thinking that Mrs Smicksmack knew some funny people, but accustomed to receiving orders, Mrs Klotz did as she was told.

'Now, bend down, dear lady and let me feel your head.'

'Feel my head? But, I'm not *ill*, Mr . . . .'

'Nebula.'

He reached out his hands and waited.

Well, thought Mrs Klotz, in for a penny, in for a pound. If he's a maniac, at least he's a polite one. She lowered her head. The large, warm hands rested upon her for a moment. It was rather comforting, if a bit peculiar. Mr Nebula closed his eyes and inhaled deeply.

'Ah, yes,' he breathed, pressing gently. 'All those worries, fears and apprehensions. Mrs Klotz, you are

indeed a deserving case.'

He released her.

'That is all I need to know.'

'Can I put my hat back on now?'

Mrs Klotz felt flattered by all this attention, but a little unsettled at the same time. Her hat gave her confidence.

'Of course, dear lady, of course. Now make yourself comfortable again and listen to my diagnosis.'

He placed the tips of his fingers together and gazed at her earnestly and tenderly from under his smoking-cap. For the first time, Mrs Klotz noticed that it was embroidered with stars.

'So, Mrs Klotz, the centre of all your troubles lies in your son, your only son, Kaspar?'

Mrs Klotz nodded.

'A strong boy, a vigorous boy, an intelligent boy, but . . . ' Mr Nebula raised a finger and Mrs Klotz followed it with her eyes, 'a heartless, ruthless, wilful, wild and disobedient boy!'

The finger descended with a thump. Mrs Klotz shook.

'Oh yes! Mr . . . .'

'Nebula.'

'Nebula. That's Kaspar all right. That's him in a nutshell!'

Mr Nebula nodded wisely then went on, 'And you, Mrs Klotz.'

'Me, Mr . . . ?'

'Nebula. Yes, you, dear lady. You have attempted to

give him all that a mother could. Without the help and support of a husband, you have cared for him, guided him and, when he strayed, pleaded with him to return to the right path. Finally, you commanded him to improve his ways. And with what result?'

Mrs Klotz was mesmerised.

'Yes, Mr Neighbourhood?'

'Nebula. With what result, I say?'

Again the finger struck the desk.

'Why, with no result whatsoever! The boy persists in his evil waywardness.'

Mrs Klotz sighed. 'Everything you say is true, Mr . . . . You'd just think that you'd known us both for years!'

He smiled mysteriously. 'Perhaps I have, Mrs Klotz. I certainly feel that it is so. And – I know more!'

Mrs Klotz edged nearer on her chair.

'A little light has begun to gleam in the darkness of your lonely life, dear lady. Shall I mention the initial "G"?'

Now she was puzzled. He couldn't mean 'gas-meter', she thought, because she hadn't paid the bill yet.

' "G" for "Grinser",' he went on. 'A chivalrous gentleman in whom you have come to place certain hopes?'

'Oh. Mr Grinser! However did you know about that?'

She reddened.

'I have my methods,' smiled Mr Nebula. 'Do not be disturbed, dear lady, I have your interests at heart.

When it comes to my clients, I am as discreet as the grave.'

I'm glad to hear it, she thought.

'And now we come to the crux of the matter. The gentleman is fond of you - you are sure of that - and your own feelings towards him are all that they should be in such a case. And yet . . . .'

'Yes?' said Mrs Klotz.

'And yet you draw back. You will not take the final plunge and listen to his generous offers because, because Mrs Klotz, you know that Kaspar in his present state would be a threat to your future happiness. And nobly, Mrs Klotz, nobly, I say, you have put aside this deserved happiness until the boy has been straightened out first!'

'Oh, Mr . . . .'

'Nebula.'

'Nebula! You're a magician! You really are. That's exactly what I'm on about - only I've never felt it so clearly in my own mind before. What can I do, Mr Nebulous? Can you help?'

Mr Nebula rose and looked down upon her kindly.

'From now on, Mrs Klotz, you will not be fighting this battle alone. Give me your hand, dear lady, and come this way.'

Mrs Klotz allowed herself to be led out of the study and found herself in a long gallery hung with silver and green brocade. Windows that reached from floor to ceiling let in a cool, gentle light down the right-hand side and on the left hung several pretty oil paintings in oval, gilt frames. Nice, she thought, as she walked on wonderingly. At the end of the gallery was an arch, but Mrs Klotz could see no further, for it was filled by a curtain of heavy, patterned velvet. Through this curtain she could hear a soft tinkling sound. Mr Nebula propelled her forwards and parted the curtains so that they might pass through.

A mechanical harpsichord, playing a delicate tune, stood against one wall. As Mr Nebula stepped across to shut it off, Mrs Klotz's gaze shot past him to the far end of the room. There, in front of a porcelain stove, painted with pink and blue flowers, stood a richly carved table and stool. At the table, seated on the stool, was an enormous, iron-grey poodle. One huge paw lay lightly on the vellum pages of an ancient book and, with the other, it held to its eye a gold-rimmed monocle on a silken ribbon. The poodle raised its head and looked at them enquiringly.

'He is so fond of music,' said Mr Nebula, turning a small lever. 'Particularly the old masters!'

Mrs Klotz had come to a halt and stood in the middle of the room. She was twisting the handles of her handbag and was experiencing a strong desire to curtsy. The poodle removed the monocle, and, after carefully marking the place in the book, climbed down heavily from the stool and waddled towards her.

'Here he is, Mrs Klotz,' said Mr Nebula, 'the Iron Poodle! He will be the constant companion of your evil boy Kaspar. He will preserve him from all temptation and wickedness and work on him, by example, to bring

him to the paths of goodness, of beauty and of truth!'

'Oh, Mr . . . ' exclaimed Mrs Klotz, collapsing on an ottoman in a heap.

'Nebula,' said Mr Nebula quietly.

And he took her by the arms and helped her up.

5

'Nonsense, Kaspar,' said Mrs Klotz airily. 'I didn't hear him say a word. Besides, poodles can't talk, can they?'

'This one can,' insisted Kaspar. 'He's doing it right now!'

Mrs Klotz paused in lifting one of Grinser's best ham bones from the soup pan and gave Kaspar a severe look. Inwardly she was rejoicing over his discomfort, but she took care not to let him see it.

'Kaspar! Any more of this and I shall call in Dr Rostipoff to have a look at you. You must have a temperature.'

Kaspar glowered at her. '*Everything's* got a temperature. That doesn't mean anything. Dead things have got a temperature – even a lump of iron's got a temperature.'

'I mean a *high* temperature. You know quite well what I'm getting at, so don't pretend you don't!'

She banged down the saucepan lid and put the steaming ham bone on a metal plate in front of the Iron Poodle. The Poodle looked up at her graciously then turned to face Kaspar's hostile glare across the table. As their eyes met, Kaspar felt the words coming again.

'What I *said*, Klotz, was, why don't you eat your bread in a civilised manner, instead of shoving it down your throat like a savage? Are you really so hungry that you need to swallow half a loaf at a time? In any case, you ought to wait for the soup.'

The Poodle slipped down off the chair and pulled open a little drawer in the sideboard. After rummaging about he returned carrying three linen napkins and laid them carefully on the table. He tucked his own neatly into his collar and indicated to Kaspar that he should do the same.

'Come along, Klotz. You've seen a napkin before. Stop looking as though you're expected to blow your nose in it.'

'Oh, look what he's doing, Kaspar!'

Mrs Klotz paused with the soup ladle in delight.

'He's trying to teach you *manners*. What a well brought up little dog. Well, go on. Put yours on too!'

'I don't want to. 'Specially after it's been in *his*

mouth. He's not so little either, unless he's some kind of little elephant.'

The Poodle looked pained.

'Come, come, Klotz. Do this small thing to please your mother.'

'Why should I want to please my mother?' bellowed Kaspar. He had had enough of this.

The Poodle's eyes narrowed.

'Shouting is a sign of weakness. Any good boy would want to please his mother. You obviously feel that you are in the wrong, so you shout to cover it up.'

'I *enjoy* being in the wrong. And I'm *not* a good boy, and I'm *not* covering anything up!'

Mrs Klotz stared hard. To Kaspar's dismay, the horror on her face seemed genuine. For a minute he was uncertain whether she was in on this game or not.

'What are you staring at? You can hear him too, can't you? I know you can't actually hear it talking out loud, but when you look at him you can hear it in your head. Can't you? Well? Can you or *can't* you?'

'I think I *will* call Dr Rostipoff. You just sit there quietly dear, and I'll bring him back in five minutes. They've got all sorts of ways of helping sick people nowadays - pills, injections, electric shocks.'

She grabbed her purse from the sideboard and opened the door. Kaspar grew desperate.

'Oh, all right!'

He brought his spoon down on the table with a crash. The Poodle's ears jerked slightly.

'I'll put the stupid thing on if it makes you happy!'

Mrs Klotz's face melted instantly into a friendly beam. 'Will you, dear? That's a good boy. I knew you'd see it my way in the end.'

The Poodle ignored her wink.

She brought the soup to the table and simpered at them both.

'Now, if we're going to do things properly in future, I'll have to get some wooden rings to hold the napkins. And then, perhaps, a little water set – you know, a nice jug with matching glasses, and a special cruet to hold the salt and pepper! I saw a lovely one in Bogdal's yesterday. All lemon pottery on a chrome base.'

Kaspar stared at her as though she'd gone mad. The Poodle, however, nodded approvingly.

'Who knows,' continued Mrs Klotz (this time at Kaspar). 'Perhaps I could teach you to set out the cutlery the way I do it at Mrs Smicksmack's. Then, laying the table could be your very own job!'

Her eyes gleamed with enthusiasm as she pictured this enterprise. Kaspar in a little white jacket? No, no she couldn't actually dress him up as a waiter. But at least a clean, white shirt and white cotton gloves, laying the silver out beautifully on a thick, white damask cloth. Kaspar with well-greased, well-brushed hair, smiling and pouring iced water from her new, crystal water set. A vase of red roses at one end; her cruet set in the centre providing a splash of contrasting colour. And at the top of the table a figure seated beside her – a figure with a moustache and a round, straw hat. Mrs Klotz looked at the Poodle in ecstasy. Life promised to be so good!

Kaspar's thoughts were somewhat different. As they sat drinking soup with their napkins on, he felt so furious with himself for giving in that he choked. He caught the Poodle's eye only with difficulty, for that animal was expressing sudden interest in the picture of a windmill stuck on the larder door. Kaspar drilled the message into him.

'In future, when you say anything to me, I will keep it to myself!'

'Very wise,' replied the Iron Poodle, giving him an equally iron look. 'And while I have your attention, would you kindly pass the salt?'

The hour that followed was one of the most painful that Kaspar had ever spent. He might have won the first skirmish with his mother by refusing to walk the Poodle and banging out of the flat before she had a chance to reply. But what satisfaction was there in that, when the next thing that happened lost him the battle?

He was not halfway down the stairs when the door was opened again. A pattering was heard behind him and, before he could *think* 'knife', much less *say* it, the Poodle was sitting at the front door, its lead lying between its paws. When he arrived at the bottom of the final flight, it yawned at him with the boredom of having to wait so long.

'Very clever,' Kaspar said, as he endeavoured to step over it. 'But from now on you're on your own!'

'We'll see about that,' replied the Poodle, lightly.

At the gate, Kaspar turned sharp right and set off at an energetic pace. He determined to ignore the Poodle at all costs and to walk the hulking brute off its fat legs. But fate intervened. As if by magic, a policeman appeared out of nowhere and bore down upon him. Thank goodness, it was not Hammelpranger.

'That your dog?'

There was hardly any point in denying it, though he would have liked to. The policeman had obviously seen them coming from the garden, and the Poodle had never left his heels for as much as a sniff. He tried his best.

'Not really. I'm just looking after it for a bit.'

'Well, in that case,' said the policeman, towering over him, 'look after it properly. Put it on the lead. I don't want it running loose near a busy road and causing an accident.'

He watched while Kaspar took the lead from the Poodle's mouth and slipped it onto the collar. He tightened it with a strong pull.

'No need to strangle him. Just make sure he keeps close,' said the policeman. He continued to watch till Kaspar was out of sight.

Kaspar was livid. At once the Avenue seemed to fill with faces he knew, all staring at him and the ridiculous dog. It wouldn't have mattered so much if only it would walk sensibly. But it didn't walk, it pranced! It lifted each leg in turn to an exaggerated height and minced by his side like a woolly ballerina. Kaspar was covered with shame.

Suddenly, he saw a crowd of boys from school some way ahead of them. Good grief! he thought. I can't let them see me out with this. They'd never let me forget it! He made a valiant attempt to alter course down a quiet back alley, but the Poodle would have none of it. He sat down obstinately and spread his paws, resisting all Kaspar's desperate wrenching on the lead. Then they were surrounded by grinning faces.

'Look here, boys! It's the great Klotz taking his doggy for a walk.'

'What a pretty doggy! What is it, Klotz, an alsatian or a wolfhound?'

Kaspar clenched his fists as they stood and laughed at him, but his red face gave him away.

'No, it's a *poodle*, isn't it, Klotz? A nice, cuddly, curly poodle. He probably takes it to bed with him!'

Several grownups turned around to look at the screeching group. Kaspar felt perspiration forming on his forehead.

'Come on you!' he muttered, tugging furiously at the lead.

'Friends of yours?' enquired the Poodle, beginning to slide along behind him gently.

'Come *on*, will you,' ordered Kaspar. His face had swollen with fury.

'Oh, very well,' said the Poodle at last. He stood and gave himself a graceful shake. 'I just didn't want to spoil your chat.'

'Look at it!' shouted the boys. 'It's grey with age and Klotz can't even move it! Do you want any help,

Klotz? Shall we give you a push?‘

The Poodle condescended to walk on. Crimson with shame, Kaspar heard the voices calling after him down the Avenue. His ears burned and for the next five minutes he never once lifted his eyes from the pavement.

After this he tried to lose it. He succeeded in persuading it to leave the main avenue and plunge into a maze of tortuous streets. At last he stopped beside a tree.

'There you are,' he said to the Poodle. 'I'll just wait around the corner while you use it.'

The Poodle looked only slightly surprised. 'That's very considerate of you. I usually pick my own trees, but this isn't a bad one.' He sniffed around the base appreciatively.

'Right,' said Kaspar. 'Don't take all day.'

As soon as he turned the corner he belted off down the street as if a hairy devil were after him. It was depressingly long and unusually straight. If he couldn't find somewhere to hide quickly, the Poodle would see him and be on his heels. He was overjoyed when, at last, he saw a little lane branching off to the left, beside some shops and a post office. He made for it breathlessly and had just turned his head to check behind, when a sigh and a well-known yawn came from the post office steps. It was the Iron Poodle.

'Excuse my not waiting for your return,' it said, 'but I know this area extremely well and I decided to take a short cut.'

Kaspar was trembling from a mixture of effort and shock. The Poodle eyed him sympathetically.

'Don't you think we should stroll along home now? Via the Avenue, I would suggest. I think I've had enough exercise for this evening and it's foolish to overdo things.'

'Perhaps it is, at your age,' retorted Kaspar (he had noticed that the Poodle was sensitive on this point), 'but I want to go further!'

'You intend to force me to go on?'

'Yes!'

'I see.'

The Poodle put his head to one side and watched him meekly. Kaspar picked up the lead. Which way now? Kaspar considered. If they went down to the river he might be able to get rid of it by pushing it in! But what if it couldn't swim?

'I can,' said the Poodle, who was calmly reading his thoughts, 'remarkably well, as a matter of fact. I have several gold medals and a challenge certificate for it.'

'Oh, come on!' Kaspar tugged him forward.

'You realise that this is against my will?'

'So what!' said Kaspar.

'Hmm,' said the Poodle.

It wasn't long before they saw an old lady coming towards them along the street. Immediately, the Poodle began to act strangely. He made frightened, whimpering noises and cowered away from Kaspar at the extreme end of his lead.

'What are you playing at?' whispered Kaspar, seeing

that the old lady had noticed this. The Poodle only whimpered and cowered with redoubled force.

'Here!' The old lady approached. 'What have you been doing to that poor dog? He's scared to death.'

'Nothing' stuttered Kaspar, 'Nothing at all – it's just . . . .'

'What's going on?'

He had not noticed the head stuck out of the second floor window above him.

'It's this poor dog,' replied the lady. 'I don't know what the boy's been doing to it, but just see how it's trembling.'

'You're right,' said the head. 'Come and look at this, Gerda. There's a dog in trouble down here.' Another head appeared, with a cigarette hanging from its lips.

'Poor little animal. He ought to be ashamed!'

Then Kaspar looked on with horror as, all down the street, faces began to poke out of windows and doorways, all anxious to find out what he'd been doing to the miserable old dog. There was a murmur about him like the buzzing of flies.

'Someone ought to do something about this,' said an unshaven man in a striped nightshirt. 'That's cruelty to animals, that is.'

A geranium pot was dislodged from a sill and fell to the cobbles with a crash. Children cried. Dogs barked. People began arguing in loud voices. Kaspar took one look down the hostile canyon and decided on retreat.

'Come on, boy,' he called cajolingly. He clicked his tongue and tried to pat the Iron Poodle on the head.

'Come on. Good dog. Let's go home.'

He took a few nervous steps and a hundred suspicious eyes followed him till he was out of sight. Away from the street, he leaned against a wall and took great breaths of air in pure relief. The Poodle sat down in front of him and caught his eye.

'Had enough?' he said.

Murder filled Kaspar's soul.

'Now, show Mrs Krug the lovely bookmark you've made!'

Old Krug sat looking at Kaspar as though a cabbage were growing out of his nose.

'He's had a *wonderful* time with that dog, Mrs Krug. Been out walking with him and then spent the rest of the evening quietly by the fire, making the marker for his bible. You wouldn't think it was the same boy!'

Old Krug sniffed. She was not a believer in instant conversions. 'Seems peaceful enough.'

'Peaceful? The whole house has been peaceful ever since that dog arrived. I can't tell you what a difference it's made, Mrs Krug. We can go out tonight and I won't have a single worry on my mind. I'll know that my Kaspar is in good hands.'

'Does that mean we won't have to hurry back?' Mrs Krug cheered up a bit. She always regretted leaving the Green Monkey before she'd had her share.

'That's right, Mrs Krug! From now on, we're free as air! Now, Kaspar – bedtime. And it's no use protesting because you know you have to go. Your new friend will

see to that. Come on, Mrs Krug. Night, night, Kaspar. See you in the morning!' He heard them talking all the way down the stairs then out into the garden.

Kaspar eyed the dog, then he made a bolt for his bedroom. If he could only get inside and shut the door before . . . But he couldn't. For all his weight, the Iron Poodle could move like a greased eel.

'Look,' said Kaspar, nearing desperation. 'Be reasonable. I've behaved myself tonight. I've done all you wanted. But now I'm going out. I've got an important meeting somewhere else and I've got to leave this house now!'

The Poodle stretched himself out on the bedside rug

and yawned widely. 'Those are not my orders,' he said.

Kaspar undid the catch on the window and, after his usual check to see that no one was looking, stuck out a leg and began to feel for the drainpipe. The Iron Poodle remained motionless.

'O.K.?' said Kaspar. 'I'm going.'

The moment his entire body disappeared from view, the Iron Poodle ambled casually towards the window and placed both paws on the ledge. He looked down calmly at Kaspar's efforts on the pipe then lifted his nose to the skies.

Kaspar was devoting all his attention to staying upright on his rickety support when, suddenly, a spine-chilling howl shattered the comparative peace of the evening.

'What the . . . ?'

Having almost lost his grip at the first shock, he clawed wildly at the drainpipe and clung on for dear life.

'Shut up, you crazy animal! You'll have half the world running here to see what's going on!'

The Poodle nodded.

'Quite correct. You've grasped the general idea immediately. Now, are you coming in off that drainpipe, or would you care for a repeat performance? I can do it much better when I really try.'

'He can't be coming now,' said Christa. 'We've waited almost an hour.'

'All right.'

Matty was reluctant to leave, but there seemed no point in staying.

'See you in the morning then.'

The little hut in the park grew silent in the silver moonlight.

6

Matty stopped swinging on the gate and stared in horror.

'What on earth is *that*?'

Kaspar was not dashing lightheartedly along the path in his usual manner. On the contrary, he trudged with the air of the convicted man who has just caught a glimpse of the block. And by his side there lolloped an extraordinary dog. Kaspar hardly looked up.

'*That*,' he said bitterly, 'is an idea of my mother's. It's supposed to keep me out of trouble.'

'You're not seriously going to walk to school with it, are you? We'll be laughed off the street!'

The Iron Poodle, who had been relishing the prospect of a brisk stroll in the sunshine, gave him a hard look. He marked Matty down as an enemy.

'Oh, let's get on with it,' groaned Kaspar. 'At the moment I haven't any choice.'

He grabbed Matty by the shoulder and whispered something in his ear.

'I've got to get rid of this gargoyle somehow. We'll talk about it at break, when he can't overhear us. Just act normally.'

The Poodle, pretending not to hear this, smiled up at him. 'Come along, Klotz. Education is a wonderful thing! And I'm looking forward to having you off my paws for an hour or two once I've left you at the gates.'

They walked on and the nightmare descended. If

Kaspar had never known up till then how few friends he had in the world, he certainly found out that morning. His worst fears were realised. Johnnie and Christa were easily dealt with. Loyalty to Kaspar at least made them sympathetic. But the others! Kaspar could only console himself by standing them up in long rows, in his imagination, and watching them fall to his machine gun. He was teased and called at unceasingly, from one end of the Schiller Avenue to the other.

The Iron Poodle rather enjoyed the attention they received. He appeared to accept it as some strange form of admiration.

'Cheerful lot, your schoolfellows, Klotz! Reminds me of the carefree days of puppyhood.'

He wagged his tail and rolled his eyes at the noisy throng around them.

The worst part came when the Poodle halted at a lamp-post. For a full minute, Kaspar closed his eyes and wished that the earth would swallow him up – or rather, that it would swallow up the hooting and giggling multitude gathered to watch the event.

'Klotz's turn next!' shrieked an oaf from Kaspar's class. Kaspar gave him a look that promised all the tortures of the Spanish Inquisition, but the boy didn't care. His joke produced a riot of laughter and he knew he was safe in the crowd.

At the gates, Christa was glad to leave them. Kaspar, Matty and Johnnie gritted their teeth and joined the boys. All three were blushing furiously. Then the Poodle signalled from the railings: 'Pick you up later.

Super walk! Got things to do now!' and galloped back up the street, ears flying. Mr Pelikan, who had watched the proceedings, decided to make a contribution to the humour of the occasion.

'Fine animal that, Klotz. But make sure it does not come into the playground. I fancy it may be a little too rough for some of our boys.'

Kaspar wondered how difficult it would be to split a man from head to foot with an ice-axe.

'All you'd have to do would be to get hold of some cats, any old cats – even one might do, and lock them in the same room as the dog.'

Johnnie's face grew excited as he outlined his plan for dealing with the Poodle.

'Then what?'

'Then the cats would get scared and start leaping all over the place, smashing things – and when your mother comes home you could say the Poodle's gone berserk. She wouldn't want to keep him after that!'

'And how do I explain away half a dozen screaming, petrified cats?'

'Well, you let them out first.'

'Without letting the Poodle out at the same time?'

Johnnie's excitement waned somewhat.

'That might be the difficult part.'

'Impossible, I should think,' said Kaspar. 'No, on the whole, I think Matty's idea was the best. How soon could you get the stuff, Matty?'

'Straight after school, if you like.'

'Right. We'll try it. And the sooner the better.'

Red-faced, Kaspar slammed the door of the flat behind him and rested against it for a few seconds to recover. Outside he still heard the voices of one or two persecutors who had run after him all the way from school.

'You were in a great hurry to get back, Klotz. I don't appreciate being rushed about like that. Especially when the children are eager to look at me. Tomorrow we will go at *my* pace!'

The Poodle stalked to an armchair and stared at him reproachfully.

'I shall study the chapter in the *Boys' Own Wonder Book of Useful Things to Know* that I have chosen to discuss with you tonight. Meanwhile, if I were you, I should have a wash!'

Kaspar looked up at the ceiling so that the Poodle couldn't see his thoughts. Matty oughtn't to be more than five minutes. Perhaps he *would* take the Poodle's advice and wash himself. As sounds of gurgling came from the bathroom the Poodle screwed in his monocle and settled down to read. The splashing sounds were agreeable to his ears. He was glad he had suggested it. Kaspar was learning some good habits at last.

Kaspar towelled himself vigorously and buttoned up his shirt. He was in no hurry to leave the bathroom, though it wasn't usually a favourite place of his. He dawdled till he heard a soft knock on the door.

The Poodle was off his chair in a flash and stuck his head into the passage. Kaspar opened the flat door and

Matty slipped him a small packet.

'No, I can't come out now, Matty,' he said in a loud voice. 'Got to get the tea ready.'

Matty winked at him and bounced off down the stairs.

'Quite right,' said the Poodle. 'We've only just got in, anyway.' He eyed Kaspar suspiciously. 'Is that all he wanted? Just for you to go out?'

Kaspar had tucked the packet up his sleeve. ''Course,' he said, and got some eggs from the refrigerator.

'Oooh! how that woman does go on!'

Mrs Klotz stretched herself in an easy chair and kicked of her shoes. Then she recollected that they had a guest in the house, even if it was only a dog. She put them on again under the Poodle's iron gaze and went to help Kaspar at the gas stove.

'I was all ready to come away at half past three when she suddenly remembered that she wanted her evening dresses ironed. Mr Smicksmack's been invited to a grand reception at the Hotel Astoria next week - something to do with the Chamber of Commerce - so naturally she wants to look her best. She's going to try them all on this evening, but I bet it's all an excuse to get Mr S. to buy her a new one!'

Mrs Klotz looked quite content banging at the saucepan so Kaspar said, 'I'll set the table, shall I?'.

The words were music to Mrs Klotz's ears. 'There now, I told you you'd enjoy it once you started. There's hidden depths in you, Kaspar. Hidden depths.' She meant it as a compliment.

Kaspar agreed. As she prattled on about the Smicksmacks and the marvellous banquet that would go on till the early hours of the morning, Kaspar got the things out of the sideboard and began to arrange them on the table. A curious look had come over his face. Twice, in hovering close to the chair where the Iron Poodle sat bent over his *Boys' Own Wonder Book*, he tapped at the little packet onto the grey, curly wool. The Poodle noticed nothing but, on the second occasion, his skin gave a slight, involuntary twitch.

'There, doesn't that smell good!' Mrs Klotz thumped a bowl of scrambled eggs and cutlets on the table and took her place hungrily.

'Come on, Mr Poodle. What's on this plate is a lot better than what's in that book, I can tell you!'

The Poodle began to lift his head to correct Mrs Klotz with a gentle smile, when suddenly, as the powder trickled down his back, he sat bolt upright and uttered a tremendous howl. All at once he fell of the chair and began scratching furiously. He snapped and growled and clawed at his coat, and rolled over and over right around the room. Eventually, he wedged himself under the table, where he could be heard moaning wretchedly.

'Kaspar, quick! He must be having a fit! Fetch Mrs Krug. Fetch Mr Grinser. Fetch Mrs Smicksmack. Fetch anybody!'

Mrs Klotz had leapt up and pulled half the crockery

off the table. The salt was falling in a steady stream onto the floor.

Kaspar remained strangely calm. 'It's all right, Mother,' he was saying. 'Keep quiet, won't you? I think I know what's happened.'

He dived under the table and saw the Poodle gnawing at his wool in concentrated fury. Then he popped up again, smiling. 'Yes, that's it. Nothing to worry about. He's just got a flea!'

For a second the Poodle was so shocked that he stopped scratching. His face registered outrage.

'How *dare* you suggest . . . ?' But the itching got the better of him before he could continue.

'A flea?' Mrs Klotz found herself going weak at the knees. A mad dog was one thing, but a dog with *fleas*? In *her* house!

'Get him out of here, Kaspar! I won't stand for it! Fleas can jump. Get him out of here and don't bring him back until he's clean!'

She retreated to a corner until Kaspar had found a stiff brush and opened the door. The Iron Poodle hurried out of the room with his tail down and with a very disagreeable expression on his face.

An hour or so later, order had returned. The Poodle was trying desperately to restore his reputation by looking as dignified as possible and pointing out things of interest in the *Boys' Own Wonder Book* to Kaspar. Mrs Klotz sat opposite, darning socks and thinking black thoughts. Every now and then she muttered, just loud enough for the Poodle to overhear, 'I don't care how useful he is. I won't have dirty, nasty fleas in here. It had better not happen again, that's all. Howling and rolling about like a lunatic.'

The Poodle was in great discomfort. Several times he tried to catch Mrs Klotz's eye to attempt an explanation. But she would never look at him for more than a second. It was infuriating. Never before had he known what it was like to be in disgrace. He felt his leg begin to twitch. Mrs Klotz stared at it. Not again! He had to control it! With super-canine willpower he forced his leg to lie quite still. Then he tried to concentrate on the chapter about 'Distress Signals used by Sailors'.

Mrs Krug flapped her handbag handles impatiently against her chest. She was being kept waiting again and all on account of a tale about some wretched flea.

'Don't you worry about it any more, dear,' she sighed. 'All animals get them occasionally. My old moggy's always chewing at himself to get rid of them.'

'Ugh!' Mrs Klotz wrinkled her nose in disgust. She had never kept animals before, except a tortoise named Albert that had wandered off after two days.

'Yes,' continued Krug, warming to her subject. 'Poor old Oscar. He does suffer at times. Specially in the winter. Why, I've seen three or four of them burrowing about on his tail. That's when they get them most, you know, in winter.'

'Oh, stop it, Mrs Krug. You're making me feel all creepy.'

'But it's nature, isn't it, dear? Yes, that's all it is. You can't do much about nature, can you?'

'Yes, I can, Mrs Krug. And I'll tell you what I can do with nature – I can shut it out!'

The Poodle's ears pricked.

'Shut it out, dear?'

'Yes, Mrs Krug. If I see any more signs of nature on that animal, even so much as a wriggle, back he goes to Mr Nebula and no mistake. He'll get his marching orders on the instant!'

From his place on the hearth-rug (where he was helping Kaspar to do his algebra) the Iron Poodle gave her an appealing look. He wanted to reassure her, to convince the poor, deluded woman that she was making a great mistake. But she would not look him in the eye. Well, he had done his best. He looked at

Kaspar and shuddered. Goodness knew what he'd get up to without the Iron Poodle on guard.

The same thought had occurred to Old Krug. 'What about, er . . . ?' The presence of Kaspar in the room made her cautious.

'What about what, Mrs Krug?' asked Mrs Klotz.

'Well, you know, dear.' Mrs Krug nodded at Kaspar's back. 'What about *him*?'

'Oh, Kaspar,' said Mrs Klotz, dropping her voice. 'He's ever so much better lately, Mrs Krug. You'd hardly believe it.'

It was obvious from Mrs Krug's expression that she certainly wouldn't.

'He hasn't been in any trouble, and he's done his homework, and he's even started helping me about the house!'

'And how long will that last?' Mrs Krug knew Kaspar of old.

'I don't know, I'm sure, Mrs Krug. But I tell you solemnly, I would take a chance on him behaving himself rather than put up with creepy crawlies. That I would. Anyway . . . .' She stood up. 'Time's getting on.'

'Heavens – just look at that clock!' said Krug in mock surprise. 'Doesn't time fly when you're having a nice chat? Still, we're in no great hurry to get back again, are we? Not so long as you keep the dog. I think it's a shame even to think of getting rid of him.'

As soon as the door had closed behind them Kaspar shut the algebra book with a snap and looked triumphantly into the Poodle's eyes.

'You and I have got something to discuss.'

'I was under the impression that we already *were* discussing something – simple equations to be precise. Now, open the book and let's get on with your homework.'

It had been a very trying evening and the Poodle spoke with more than a hint of impatience. But Kaspar was not daunted.

'This is more important than algebra. That is, if you consider staying on in this house *is* important?'

The Poodle did not like the knowing manner in which Kaspar said this.

'Staying on in this house? Well, of course I am staying on, you foolish boy. I shall remain here until I have succeeded in my task, as usual, or until my orders take me elsewhere . . . .'

'Or,' interrupted Kaspar.

'There is no other "or",' snapped the Iron Poodle. 'I have indicated the only . . . .'

Again, Kaspar did not wait for him to finish. '*Or* – until you are attacked by fleas again and my mother turfs you out!'

The Poodle drew himself up to his full size (which was considerable) and breathed in sharply. 'What took place this afternoon was as untypical as it was inexplicable. Never in my life have I been anywhere in the neighbourhood of a flea and it is not my intention to strike up a friendship with one now. It is true that the circumstances of life compel me to occupy the same universe, the same planet even, as the creature you mention. But by the same token, I exist in a world of people, yaks and emus. It would be just as likely to find my beautiful fur infested by leaping hippopotamuses, as the particular form of biological horror you suggest. Besides, I bathe two or three times a day with a rather expensive shampoo and lotion. No flea so bold as to approach me would survive for an instant!'

'Then it's lucky,' said Kaspar, 'that I don't have to bother with real fleas.'

The Poodle's expression changed.

'Bother with real fleas? *Bother* with . . . ?'

'All I wanted to do,' continued Kaspar, 'was to make you *act* as though you had them so that my mother would believe it. And you did. You acted beautifully!'

With the air of a magician at a party, Kaspar slid the little packet out of his sleeve. The Iron Poodle adjusted his monocle and leaned forward to read it.

'Krazy Arthur's Itching Powder. Hours of Agony Guaranteed. Amuse any Friends You've Got Left!!'

'What is this?' He frowned thoughtfully for a moment. Then, realisation struck him like a sock on the jaw. 'Klotz! You monster! You degenerate, shameless bandit! You mindless gastropod!'

The glass in his monocle cracked under a fierce clench from his eye-muscles. 'Do you mean to say that *you* were the cause of that excruciating torment? That whole disgraceful and degrading episode? That shocking stain on my honour and character?'

'Bull's-eye,' said Kaspar, stepping back quickly.

'And you'd better not get over-excited. The packet's not empty yet!' He rattled it ominously.

The effect was immediate. The Poodle postponed his intended plan of launching himself at Kaspar with the hairbrush and merely dug his claws a little deeper into the hearth-rug.

'You pirate, Klotz! You boil! You drain blocked up by dish-rags! You . . . .'

'All right, all right. Don't bother to go on. You'll only wear out your brain. Now, it's your turn to listen to me. We're going to make a little deal. And if you don't agree to do what I've decided, you'd better start packing your bags!'

7

Old Krug's cat, Oscar, was lying on his back on the path, sunbathing. He was also waiting for the milkman. This custom dated from his far-off infancy, when he hadn't supported enough marmalade fur to cover a slice of bread. The acrobatics of a pair of cabbage-white butterflies had brought him onto the path at full pelt, intent on slaughter. Mr Zwingli, the yodelling milkman, had been approaching at the same time.

The resulting collision had produced slight bruising in the port side ribs for Oscar and three weeks hobbling about with a sprained ankle for the milkman. But, more importantly, as a result of this encounter, a bottle of the MooCow Dairy's luscious product had fallen like a bomb from Mr Zwingli's basket. It had splattered Oscar (who was seeking refuge in a clump of dock leaves) with an unexpected white rain, apparently from heaven. He had gorged himself on the spilt milk until his stomach came down further than his legs. And now, although he had become a middle-aged cat, and was not quite so certain as he had been about heaven, he still regarded milkmen and butterflies as varieties of angel who might, if he hung around long enough, produce rewards of his favourite liquid.

He wriggled slightly from time to time, for, although the path was hot (which was the way he liked it) he had carelessly chosen a gritty part, and he was too lazy to move. He folded his paws across his chest and half-opened one eye to look at the birds. What a racket they made! ‘A bird in the mouth is a cat’s best friend.’ Was that right? Something like that. It was too warm to think. He couldn’t care. The words of psalm 17 floated through his mind. ‘They are enclosed in their own fat: with their mouth they speak proudly.’ How true, thought Oscar. His whiskers twitched.

Kaspar heaved himself up in bed that morning with a sensation of relief. If he had been ninety years old, he would have felt eighty years younger.

The sunbeams seemed to be hammering on the windowpanes with unusual ferocity. So he slid out from under the feather bolster and let them in. The air smelt good. A light, tangy breeze carried over from the river and the petrol fumes of the Schiller Avenue added an interesting flavour of their own. The clouds were away on holiday, the sparrows and starlings were chirping and twittering and, looking down into the garden, Kaspar saw that all was in readiness for one of his favourite games. It was a simple game, but it gave much pleasure. He kept a jar of pebbles especially for the purpose. He reached for it and began to unscrew the lid.

‘What was that!’

Oscar lurched out of sleep into a pose of businesslike ferocity. If one of those birds had been dropping rubbish on him it had better watch out! He licked roughly at the place where the pebble had stung him. Then he sighed and sank back.

Possibly it had been a small twig. Birds seemed to enjoy carrying them about. It must exercise their beaks.

Kaspar waited until he looked quite settled again and launched another stone. His aim was world-famous. Oscar spat. It was amazing, truly amazing, but three times out of four when he chose to spend a sunny morning dozing on the path and waiting for the angel, this phenomenon would occur! Things would strike him - apparently from nowhere - but making the final part of their journey through the sky. Perhaps it was some form of meteoric shower? He swished his tail. Around him, all was peaceful. Green grass. Blue sky. The occasional ant. He blinked. Was it worthwhile making an attempt to slumber here? Or should he curl up in the old pail in the shed? Kaspar settled the matter by deluging him with a small handful of grit.

Oscar began the trek. He found it impossible to understand the motives of God. On the occasion when he had been attempting the murder of the butterflies he had been awarded the milk from the sky. Yet now, when all he wanted was innocent sleep, an avalanche of rock was hurled upon his head. He paused before he took the corner. Did the birds suffer from this? he wondered.

Matty looked surprised when he saw the Poodle accompanying Kaspar to the gate.

'Didn't it work?' he whispered anxiously.

'Oh, yes. It worked all right.' Kaspar never gave

everything away at once.

At the end of the garden wall the Poodle stopped.

'This is it,' said Kaspar, with some relish. 'The parting of the ways.'

He undid the Poodle's lead and gave it to him.

'What you do from now on is your own business. And what *I* do is *mine*. Just be sure you meet me where I said at half past three, and no monkey tricks!'

The Poodle looked at him coolly. 'Have it your own way, Klotz. But I warn you: this will bring nothing but trouble.'

Kaspar laughed his most disagreeable laugh. The Poodle made his exit.

'Where's he going?' asked Matty.

'What do I know or care – as long as it's not with us! Come on!'

There was a good deal of disappointment from the other children who walked to school along the Avenue. They had been expecting a comedy act like the day's before. But seeing that Kaspar now had both hands free they kept their distance, while he and Matty amused themselves by walking on the heels of the unwary.

Christa and Johnnie met them with signs of relief. Kaspar had bounced back into their esteem.

'Does this mean that everything's all right again?'

'Sure,' Kaspar said. 'I'll give the details later.'

At school, Mr Pelikan shared the disappointment of his pupils. He raised a pudgy hand to quell the murmuring of the boys and gazed at the gates regretfully.

'I hope nothing unpleasant has befallen that friendly dog of yours, Klotz? It was a very welcome addition to your entourage.'

Kaspar did not choose to interpret this as a question.

'He has not met with an accident I hope?'

Kaspar smiled. 'No, Mr Pelikan.'

'Then where is he this morning? Is he feeling unwell?'

'No, Mr Pelikan. The police said it was too dangerous for him to go home on his own. So I decided it would be better not to bring him.'

Murmurs of disbelief greeted the conclusion of this lie.

'Really, Klotz? I am surprised. I was under the impression that the poodle was bringing *you*!'

The ripple of laughter among the boys seemed to satisfy Mr Pelikan. He stepped back and Myrmidon got on with the register.

'I shouldn't at all wonder,' said Miss Nesselfieber to Miss Poltergeist, 'if that poor animal isn't in a sack at the bottom of the river by now.'

Miss Poltergeist's pop eyes grew poppier.

Having tucked his lead carefully out of sight, the Iron Poodle paced the streets sadly. There was only one thing to be done, but he hated to do it. He must report back to base immediately and seek further orders.

It injured his pride to admit that he had been outfoxed by the boy Klotz, but pride must sometimes be swallowed and this was one of those times. He turned the matter over in his mind several times but still had come to no solution when he entered Prince's Street. So, determined to state the facts just as they were (devil take them) he went in through the portals of number 97.

There he met with a shock. Pinned to the door of 97b was a notice. He sat up on his hind legs to get a better view. The notice was hand-printed in black ink in Mr Nebula's microscopic, gothic script. It read:

'Called away on urgent occult business. Expect to return in three weeks. No milk. No newspapers. No circulars. Thank you!

Nebula.'

He sat down heavily and uttered an un-iron groan. Three weeks! Was he going to have to put up with this blackmail for almost a month? He couldn't bear it! What was Mr Nebula thinking of – to leave him on such a case with no reinforcements? It was insupportable! He sniffed disconsolately. Then he looked at the door. Well, at least he was home again. And he needed time to think.

Mr Nebula's apartment door was surrounded by a beautiful casing of green and white marble. Some of the green bits stuck out in bumps. The Iron Poodle pressed one of these at nose-level and heard the door give its usual 'click'. He went in and closed it behind him. It was still and dark. The clocks had stopped and the shutters were closed.

'Ah!' he breathed. 'No reek of frying sausages! No Mrs Klotz prattling incessantly about the Smicksmacks. No Mrs Krug impatiently banging her handbag on everything. And, above all, no Kaspar with his wretched packet of itching powder!'

He wandered down to his own salon and snuffled the beloved objects. Books, vases, mirrors, tapestries; how he had missed them! He went across to the automatic harpsichord and inserted his favourite music-roll, a set of Variations by Mozart. Then he sat down in an armchair upholstered in soft yellow velvet and closed his eyes. For a few moments, he and Mozart could be alone together. He felt almost happy.

'Aaarghh! You murd . . . Bloop!'

Lecker's head disappeared for the sixth time into the washbasin. Kaspar glanced around warily. Revenge had to be quick on school premises. The cloakroom was empty but one or two boys had poked their heads in to see who was getting it and the news would soon be about.

'O.K. Let go his arms. Let him up.'

Lecker came up, spouting like a grampus, and staggered against the coat-pegs.

'Enjoy your wash, Lecker?'

'You certainly needed it,' said Johnnie.

'Especially your tongue,' Kaspar said. 'That was for laughing at me yesterday morning. I didn't forget. Keep out of my way in future, unless you want more.'

The three strode out into the playground. Boys stood and stared at them from a safe distance, the way that a herd of antelope or wildebeeste will calmly watch the lioness once she has selected her prey. But Mr Myrmidon noticed nothing. With his nose stuck in a copy of *Our Winged Friends* and his hand clutching a cup of hot coffee he had enough to do just to walk about.

They found their usual place (the steps leading down to the boiler-room), sat down, and made themselves comfortable. Matty passed round a tube containing chunks of pink bubblegum, so conversation ceased until they had worked it into the right condition.

'So?' asked Johnnie, who was still somewhat behind

with the news.

'So?' Kaspar replied, more interested in the bubblegum.

'So what's happening about the dog?'

The Iron Poodle's absence was welcome, but it was still unexplained.

Kaspar was busy inflating the gum. He waited until he had scraped the mess off his face and rolled it back into his mouth before replying. 'The dog's no problem.' He chewed some more. 'Matty's powder worked like magic.' Matty grinned. 'So,' continued Kaspar, 'the dog's seen sense. I behave myself when I'm at home and pretend it's because of his good influence. And he doesn't bother us on the way to and from school, and he comes out with us at night. Otherwise he gets the powder.'

He tried a bigger bubble.

'Why's he got to come out with us at night?'

'That's part of the bargain.'

'Yes, but why?'

''Cause we can give him a job. I thought he might take the can around for us and then you could do more singing.'

'Oh,' said Johnnie. He wasn't sure that he was keen on this move.

'It's for the best,' said Kaspar sternly. 'Audiences like a change. Otherwise they don't cough up. You've no objection, have you?'

'Me? No! I've no objection. No. None at all. Not real objections. It's just . . . .'

'Good,' said Kaspar, pocketing his gum.

Old Schwanker appeared on the steps with a hand-bell and Myrmidon looked up thankfully. Break was over.

'Let's go,' said Kaspar.

On the way into class he stuck the bubblegum carefully on the seat of Miss Nesselfieber's chair.

Having decided that all he could do for the moment was drift with the tide, the Iron Poodle made only token resistance when Kaspar told him that he was to collect money in a can.

'I see,' he said.

'Is that all?' said Kaspar.

The Poodle gave him a doleful look. 'In your usual charitable manner you do not leave me very much choice.'

'That's right.'

Kaspar was making a bee-line for the window when he stopped, all at once, in his tracks.

'Of course! No need to go this way any more! You know, no doubt, where my mother keeps the spare key?'

The Poodle's brain whirled into activity. Was there a dim chance to escape this dreadful ordeal? After all, it wasn't going to be easy getting *him* along a drainpipe!

'Spare key?' he said vaguely. 'To the flat door you mean? Hmm. No, I don't think . . . .'

'Come on!' Kaspar could sound very harsh at times. 'Don't fool about!' He produced the packet from his shorts and waved it threateningly. The whirling in the Poodle's brain stopped. The case was hopeless. 'This way,' he said, wearily.

Later that night they were on their way to Coffee Nickel's. Thanks to Grinser's pig, Johnnie's extra song and the collecting efforts of the Iron Poodle, they were carrying quite a hoard.

The Iron Poodle's feelings were curiously mixed. Having been born in a silk-lined basket, he felt rather touched at the determined way these poor children had set out to earn money. The Street Theatre of Konings-haven, hmm. Was it such a very evil idea really? No. But think of the anxiety of the parents! Think of the dangers to young children running about unprotected at night! This could not be allowed to continue! But, on the whole, he concluded, if they really *must* come out, then it was a good idea of his to stay with them. (He had always found theatricals rather fun.) At the same time he was very glad that Mr Nebula was not there to see him.

The conversation buzzed on. He hardly heard it. He felt tired. A good job, he thought, that Mrs Klotz no longer checked Kaspar's bedroom when she returned. Her trust in him caused a slight pang of conscience.

Now that the excitement of the performances was over, Christa was not feeling very happy. They had avoided most of their usual pubs, but coming down to Coffee Nickel's seemed an unnecessary danger.

'Couldn't we go somewhere else to get something to

eat, Kaspar? We know Rudolf's gang use this place and I don't see why they should get any of our money.'

'That's occurred to me already. But we're later than usual, so they may not have hung about. Anyway, we'd probably have to walk miles to find anywhere similar.'

'That's right,' said Johnnie. 'We can scout around at the weekend for a new coffee place, but let's risk it tonight.'

Nevertheless, they did not walk straight out onto the quayside, but stood in the gloom for a while, watching. One or two people passed by. Some were sailors rolling drunkenly back to the ships. But there was no sign of Rudolf.

'Seems O.K.,' said Matty.

The aroma of hot coffee curled into the Iron Poodle's nostrils, and woke him up. Not fully – but just into a state of pleasant drowsiness. He was completely invisible under the seat. For one thing they were sitting in deep shade and for another he was screened by a row of eight legs. Would they never go home, those eight legs? And there again, could he face the walk?

He had turned over with difficulty (there was a lot of him to turn and not much space) and was just dropping off to sleep again, when he heard footsteps approach and then stop. Something curious in the atmosphere made him suddenly alert. In the darkness under the bench he opened his eyes.

'Business first, small talk later. Hand it over,' said Rudolph.

Kaspar gave him the tin without a word. The others looked on glumly.

'You won't mind if we take a little *more* than half, will you? After all, we've missed you this last night or two.'

None of Kaspar's bunch spoke. It was just too disheartening.

Rudolph smiled. 'They don't seem very chatty, do they, lads? They must be tired out after their hard work. Come on. Let's leave them to it.'

The three thugs turned to go but something occurred to Rudolph and he swivelled slowly on his heel.

'Tell me, K. Klotz. Has your good mother mentioned the banquet they're holding at the Hotel Astoria next week?'

Kaspar nodded slowly, longing to get rid of them.

'Did she happen to say if the Smicksmacks would be there?'

'They've been invited,' said Kaspar. 'I expect they're going.'

'Hmm. Nice for them, eh? Never mind. Save up and you'll be able to eat at the Astoria yourself some day. So long. Keep up the good work.'

'They're rotten, just rotten!' said Christa. 'I wish you hadn't given them a penny!'

'You know what they'd do if I hadn't paid up. There was nothing else for it. We've just got to keep out of their way in future. We can't come to Coffee Nickel's again.'

The Poodle, who had emerged from under the bench, laid a paw on Kaspar's knee. He had been taking great note of the discussion and an iron look had returned to his face.

'Avoid Rudolph's gang and abandon Coffee Nickel's? Not necessarily, Klotz,' he said confidently. 'Not necessarily.'

8

It wasn't often that Mrs Klotz felt seriously grieved about her lot in life. She enjoyed a good grumble as much as the next person, but she never brooded for long. Her mind was always flitting about from one thing to another, like her blue feather duster. Considering that she had her living to earn, and a millstone like Kaspar round her neck, she could even be described as moderately cheerful. But there were times when she realised that a yawning gap lay between what she would like to enjoy and what she could actually afford. The gap made one of its more impressive yawns as soon as Mrs Smicksmack lifted the lid of the cardboard box.

The lid bore the label of Messrs. Sprottfinger and Gickler, the most expensive dress shop on the fashionable Konings Avenue.

'He *insisted*, Mrs Klotz, positively *insisted* that I couldn't think of going to dinner at the Astoria in one of my old evening gowns. "Smicksmack," I told him, "I have thirty-seven evening dresses, some of which I haven't even worn already! Why should you throw away good money on buying me another!"' She parted the tissue paper and lifted up the garment for Mrs Klotz to admire.

'But you know what he's like where I am concerned Mrs Klotz. So extravagant! Do you know, he wanted to buy me two. Just in case I'd gone off the first one when I'd got it home! Such recklessness. Such generosity.'

Mrs Klotz gazed at the beautiful dress and imagined herself in it. The material was grey silk and it was decorated around the neck with hundreds of tiny seed-pearls. What a waste, she thought, for a woman who has thirty-seven others. Most of the people Mrs Klotz knew parted with money the same way they parted with teeth. They did it at the last possible moment and with the greatest reluctance. All Mrs Smicksmack had to do was pout a little and say she was bored and Mr Smicksmack's cigar drooped thirty degrees in panic while his hand reached for the fat wallet in his inside pocket!

'I think I should have my hair tinted to go with it. What would you say, Mrs Klotz? A pale mauve, possibly?'

Mrs Smicksmack sat down at her dressing table and twisted her head about to examine it in the mirror.

'Pale mauve's very nice,' agreed Mrs Klotz, (Match your face, dear, she thought.)

'Or, perhaps,' said Smicksmack pensively, picking at it with her fingers, 'a vivid orange? That would be rather striking, wouldn't it?'

'Oh, very striking, Mrs Smicksmack. And it would go well with your green eyes.' (Just like a cat's, she added under her breath.)

'But no. No. I'll stick to my first idea! First ideas are usually best, Mrs Klotz. Especially in artistic matters.'

'I'm sure you're right, Mrs Smicksmack.'

'I'm *sure* I am, Mrs Klotz. Now, fetch me my jewel case, will you? I think I left it somewhere in the drawing room. Or the sun lounge, perhaps? Oh, no! I remember now. I carried it into the kitchen last night when I was giving pussy her cod. I think, incidentally, that we must try a new fishmonger. Pussy didn't like it at all.'

Mrs Klotz eventually found the jewel case in the bathroom. It was lying under a box of Turkish delight and a pile of magazines. A fortune in jewels left lying around like that, she thought. Anybody could just walk in and take the lot. Then Mrs Smicksmack would be sorry. They'd cost a bit more than a few evening dresses to replace!

She returned with the case to the dressing room and watched as the catch was undone. A higgledy-piggledy heap of gems sparkled up from the black velvet.

'Moonstones, Mrs Klotz?' said Mrs Smicksmack. 'Or would rubies go better with the dress?'

Mrs Klotz sighed.

Matty's accordion played sweetly as the Iron Poodle frisked around with the tin. He wasn't quite prepared to admit it yet, but he was beginning to find these evenings out rather fun. True, he thought the children's performances somewhat amateurish. And he was determined, once he had gained their confidence, to give them a few useful tips. But taking round the tin wasn't half as bad as he had expected. He had made particular friends with some of the customers at the Corrugated Dolphin, who regularly slipped him lumps of cheese. And when the rest of the audience were feeling stingy, he found that he only had to sit on his hind legs and put his head on one side to stimulate their generosity. Human beings were very simple creatures, he reflected.

More importantly, he was looking forward to seeing how his plan for dealing with Rudolf's gang would work out. Kaspar hadn't really believed that he wanted to help at first, and Matty, Johnnie and Christa were even more sceptical. But he would show them! An Iron Poodle was someone to be trusted. Someone who could be relied upon.

Johnnie's last song was just ending so he emptied the tin into a cloth bag containing the rest of the evening's takings and set off on the final assault. The tearful crowd left it full to the brim and the Poodle returned to the group with an aching jaw.

'Thank goodness that's over,' he said to Kaspar. 'I'm almost fit to drop.'

'I hope you've still got *some* energy left,' Kaspar replied. 'Remember what you said you'd do tonight?'

'Have no fear about that, dear boy. An Iron Poodle keeps his word. Did I never tell you my family motto: "Mud and Iron"?'

'What does the "Mud" part stand for?'

'I couldn't say,' blinked the Iron Poodle, absentmindedly. 'Something to do with doormats, I believe.' He shook the rest of the money into the bag.

Just then, Christa stepped forward. She had been talking quietly with Johnnie a little distance away and

it appeared that they had come to some sort of decision.

'Kaspar,' she announced, 'Johnnie and I want to take our share of the money and go home now. We don't want to go down to the waterfront!'

Kaspar stared at her.

'It seems stupid to us, doesn't it, Johnnie? Giving away half of what we earn every night to those crooks. We're fed up with it!'

Kaspar said nothing.

'Well?' persisted Christa. 'Can we have it now, or not?'

Johnnie edged nearer, forgetting to hobble on his crutch. He looked first at Kaspar, then he fixed on Matty. 'What about you, Matty? Do you agree with us?'

His voice was very low. He seemed a little ashamed of himself. Slowly Matty turned his back on him and began to whistle quietly.

'There's the bag,' said Kaspar. 'Help yourself.'

He handed it over to Christa. She counted what was inside and gave some to Johnnie, who didn't seem to know what to do with it. He fumbled to get it into his pocket and then stood uncertainly.

'Why don't we all just go home?' he said. 'Just for once?'

'No thanks,' replied Kaspar. 'Some of us don't run away as soon as the going gets rough.'

He took the bag from Christa, picked up his things and set off down the street with Matty and the Poodle. Matty turned to say something to him, but Kaspar silenced him with a shake of the head.

'Keep walking,' he said.

They turned the corner of the street, leaving Christa and Johnnie alone in the lamplight. Thirty seconds later they heard footsteps running after them. Johnnie, followed by a very grumpy-looking Christa fell into step alongside.

'Changed my mind,' he said.

'Oh?' said Kaspar.

The five walked on in silence.

'Pies tonight?' said Coffee Nickel. 'And two extra! You lot must have worked up quite an appetite.'

The hurricane lamp hissed cheerfully as he wrapped them up and poured the coffee. They crunched their way back to a bench, but not to the one they usually occupied. The new bench was a little further away from the coffee stall and they had been obliged to clear it of the old newspapers a tramp had been using as an eiderdown. Its big advantage, which Kaspar spotted immediately, was that the nearest streetlight wasn't working, so that it stood in the deepest gloom.

'Very thoughtful of you,' said the Iron Poodle, making short work of the two hot pies. 'Now, I'll just get into the trees behind you and you can leave the rest to me.'

He settled down behind the trunk of a big lime and laid his nose on his paws.

'Don't you go to sleep!' whispered Kaspar. 'Remember we're depending on you!'

The Iron Poodle gave a contented snort.

Higher up the quay there was a bustle of activity as a brightly-lit cargo vessel prepared for a night sailing. They could see the customs officer's white cap as he strode down the gangway, which he helped to unfasten and shove back aboard. A small tug curvetted up to pull the ship out into the midstream and they saw men running about and shouting while the tow-lines were made fast. The mooring cables were slipped and the anchor upped. A low, solemn blast made their flesh tingle. The man at the wheelhouse window, which was the only one not to have curtains, waved to the customs officer as the boat swung out. The customs man mounted his bicycle and pedalled off to his office, where, no doubt, there was a hot stove and a glass of schnapps.

The boat slid past them on the night-tide. Kaspar couldn't make out the legend on the stern, but she flew a foreign flag. A coaster, he thought, going home to Esbjerg or Copenhagen, or on to the Baltic ports. He tried to imagine what it was like to sail about in a familiar world and then to step out into a strange land, where the sounds and smells were different. He was brought back to reality as Matty gave him a nudge in the ribs.

Three figures were heading towards them from the direction of the coffee stall. It was impossible to make out these figures but their shambling walk announced their identity.

'Sit tight,' murmured Kaspar. 'Let me do the talking.' The thugs loomed up.

'Well, well, well,' leered Rudolf. 'What a surprise. I thought you might be taking a little rest tonight after working so hard yesterday. Did you think we wouldn't spot you – sitting here all cosy in the dark?'

'We never thought about it,' said Kaspar coolly.

His manner irritated Rudolf. 'I'll bet you didn't. Dodging us never crossed your minds, eh?'

'Not at all,' Kaspar replied. 'It isn't very important. Look,' he added, 'the tug's going back downstream.'

Matty, Johnnie and Christa pretended to follow his gaze with great interest. In reality, they were terrified.

'Right! That's enough of your cheek. This is business. Remember? And it's going to cost you more if you try to play games with me. Now, let's have the money.'

Kaspar was holding the bag but he didn't budge. He just went on looking quietly at the river.

'Give me the bag!' ordered Rudolf, moving closer to him. 'Unless you want some trouble.'

They sat motionless and tense. Suddenly, Kaspar said, 'We've decided not to pay you any more. If you want money, you'll just have to work for it like anybody else. Why don't you get lost?'

'What? You little . . . .' Rudolf was outraged. 'Right, lads, if that's the way he wants it, we'll shake it out of him. Get him!'

Ferdy and Ernst sprang forward. This was a job they liked.

'O.K. Now show the little . . . .'

But what they were going to show Kaspar, no one had time to find out. A blood-curdling howl went up in the trees behind them and a pair of red eyes glowed in the blackness.

'My dog,' smiled Kaspar. 'He can't bear anyone touching me.

A ferocious scrabbling sound began, accompanied by wild barking. Ferdy and Ernst took one look at each other and took to their heels like twin comets. They couldn't see the beast in the darkness, but it sounded enormous! With Rudolf panting to keep up with them they didn't slacken off till they had vanished from the waterfront. Christa, Matty and Johnnie leapt up and hooted after them in triumph as the Iron Poodle, a little out of breath, emerged from behind his tree.

'Hooray! No more skulking about and hiding and

keeping out of their way!'

'Hooray! No more handing out our money. Everything we make is ours to keep!'

'Hooray for the Poodle! Well done, boy!'

Kaspar sat smiling at them like a tribal chieftain at a jamboree. The dog certainly had his uses. Nobody could deny it now. And nobody would again challenge Kaspar's decisions as head of the gang. Not after what had just happened. His satisfaction was complete.

The Poodle was hugged, squeezed and mauled with gratitude. Eventually, he found it rather wearying.

'Thank you, thank you,' he puffed. 'But *do* control yourselves! Remember that I am quite accustomed to success and find demonstrations of this kind unnecessary. Now, before you all become hysterical and jump in the river, gather round. I have another little surprise for you!'

Gottfried Pottelnuss – thin, crew-cut and bespectacled – climbed into the chauffeur-driven Prunk-Benz and waved a pale hand at Mr Pelikan. He was the son of Carl-Otto Pottelnuss, owner of the famous Pottlenuss Fish Paste factories, and was the only pupil whom Pelikan ever bothered to escort across the playground. He was allowed to leave school five minutes early every day, for he had a delicate constitution (despite the fish paste) and Mr Pelikan did not want him to be jostled by the crowd. Kaspar always watched the procedure with interest from his desk by the window, not because he found Gottfried Pottelnuss an impressive figure, but because he was fascinated by the car. Such a car, long, blue and gleaming, played a leading part in his private fantasy life. In the final lesson, which usually consisted of Nesselfieber and a map, he would alternately pursue round-the-world expeditions in it or use it for bank hold-ups.

He looked up quickly. Nesselfieber had just addressed a question to him ending in the word 'Florida'. His blank, grey eyes came to rest on her teeth.

'Sorry, Miss Nesselfieber?'

The bell rang.

'Oh, never mind. Stupid boy! You may go. You may *all* go,' she added irritably.

She snatched up the map and pressed it to her bony chest. Enough was enough for one day, she thought.

The school disgorged its occupants onto the street. As the briefcase-swinging, pushing, chattering mob advanced, cats slipped quietly around corners and old ladies who had been sleeping peacefully behind net curtains shut their windows with a bang.

The children rattled down the street like a mountain stream and, at the Schiller Avenue, split up into ones, twos and threes to go their separate ways. Kaspar, Matty, Johnnie and Christa did not split up. They had an appointment to keep which made them both excited and curious. The Poodle had invited them to visit the apartment where he normally lived and had promised that they would find something there to their interest and advantage.

'But these things are beautiful – just beautiful,' breathed Christa. 'We couldn't possibly use them!'

'Nonsense, dear girl,' the Poodle replied. 'They are simply wasting away at the moment and Mr Nebula (a momentary chill seized his heart when he thought of him), Mr Nebula has rooms full of such stuff.'

They were standing in a little wood-panelled chamber filled with curious cabinets and life-sized figures in strange costumes. An old, carved chest stood open before them. It was overflowing with theatrical gear; velvet cloaks, painted masks, swords, wigs and crowns; strings of false pearls, ostrich plumes and coloured handkerchiefs. There was even a tiny folding table with a hole in the bottom for producing rabbits out of hats.

'Yes,' went on the Poodle. 'I see no harm in it at all. Mr Nebula (he felt the chill again) will not be returning for at least two weeks, so we can use it quite freely until then. Everything can be returned to the box each night and no one will know where it comes from. Anyway, I have become rather bored with collecting the money and I wish to display my talents a little.'

He placed a conical wizard's hat over his topknot and tapped it with a wand.

Soon they were making so much money that Kaspar suggested they should open a bank account.

'It seems stupid not to make the money work for us. Just think of all the interest it would earn!'

'Hmm, good idea,' agreed the Iron Poodle.

'Though, purely to satisfy my curiosity, can you tell me what you want all this money *for*?'

Kaspar looked at him in surprise. 'Isn't that obvious?' he asked.

The Poodle shook his woolly head. 'No, dear boy, it is not! Unless you want to build a real theatre, or found an orphanage or something?'

'Nothing so complicated. We all have the same ambition. That's what brought us together in the first place. We simply want to make so much money that we'll be able to retire as soon as we leave school and spend the rest of our lives enjoying ourselves.'

The Poodle put his head to one side and raised his eyebrows. 'How *shrewd*,' he said. 'I wish *I'd* thought of that. And if our luck keeps up for a little longer, you may very easily succeed!'

'Note, dear,' said Mrs Krug. 'I can see it sticking out of your letterbox.'

'Funny, at this time of night,' mused Mrs Klotz, for they had just returned from the Green Monkey and it was well after eleven o'clock.

'I'll come up with you and see what it's about, shall I, dear?' Mrs Krug loved a mystery.

'If you like,' Mrs Klotz replied. 'I don't know what it can be, I'm sure.'

She unfolded the grubby piece of paper and looked at the bottom. It was signed 'A Friend'. Grinser? she wondered, but the paper was so dirty that she couldn't believe it was from him. Besides, he'd only left them five minutes ago.

'What's it say, dear? Read it out.'

Mrs Krug hung onto her arm.

'It says – just a minute – it's terrible writing, "If you want to find Kaspar don't look in his bedroom. Try in front of the Mermaid and Lobster in Cocoa Lane!" '

The Iron Poodle had just completed the difficult manoeuvre of producing a green hen's egg from his nose when a faint shriek was heard somewhere at the back of the crowd. Yes, he thought, that one usually makes quite an impression. But as the crowd parted he saw that he was quite mistaken. Kaspar's group of entertainers found themselves looking at the horrified face of old Mrs Krug and, beside her, the figure of Kaspar's mother, Mrs Klotz, slumped up against a lamp-post and with her best black hat knocked rakishly over one eye.

9

'I've *said* it and I *mean* it. That is the last meal he's ever going to eat in this house! So now, if you're ready, Mr Poodle, we'll be on our way.'

Mrs Klotz bustled to the door and stood there holding the Poodle's lead with every sign of impatience. Kaspar, at the breakfast table, thought he'd better try to look upset, as this was obviously what Mrs Klotz expected. But this was very difficult, because he knew perfectly well that Mr Nebula had not returned yet and so his mother would be compelled to bring the Poodle back.

'Hurry up, *please*,' she said, fidgeting with the lead. Kaspar and the Iron Poodle looked at one another and Kaspar shrugged his shoulders. There was no point in trying to explain to Mrs Klotz about Mr Nebula's notice. In the first place she wouldn't believe him and would insist on seeing it for herself, and secondly, it would only start another row, and Kaspar had had enough of that already. He dunked his bread and jam into the coffee and took a bite.

''Bye, Poodle,' he murmured sadly with his mouth full.

'Goodbye, Klotz,' the Poodle said aloud, then whispered, 'The walk will do her good!'

Kaspar's gang strolled in a huddle down the Avenue.

'So you see,' he was saying, 'she's got no option but to

bring him back. Then we'll just have to wait till she calms down and forgets about it.'

'But by that time Mr Nebula's bound to have returned,' groaned Johnnie. 'And then we'll lose the Poodle for good!'

'That's a possibility. But don't give in yet. I'll think of something. We've got too much invested in that dog to give him up without a fight.'

They trudged around the corner and saw the school gates. Its metal bars looked like the teeth of a hungry monster waiting to devour them.

The Poodle stood aside courteously to allow Mrs Klotz to enter the building first.

'Very impressive,' she remarked bitterly, 'but I've seen what your good manners amount to!'

She grasped the bell handle and gave it a good tug. A faint ringing penetrated into the hall. She was in such a state that it took several minutes before she observed the notice.

'Now what?' she muttered, peering at it. 'Urgent occult business – expect to return in three weeks.' The situation registered.

'Three weeks!'

She sat down on a hall chair and stared into space. Unpleasant visions obviously possessed her. After tracing a few patterns on the marble floor with his left hind foot, the Poodle coughed discreetly and glanced up at her. The red spot near her adam's apple was glowing brightly.

'Right!' she announced suddenly. 'Right!' She stood up smartly and glared at him. 'No one could accuse me of being cruel to animals so I'll see that you don't starve for the next three weeks. But at the end of that time we're coming here again and on *that* occasion,' she wagged a finger at him, 'on *that* occasion I'll get you into this flat supposing I have to push you through the keyhole!'

The red spot burned like the cone of a volcano.

Mrs Smicksmack looked in the mirror for the eighth time that morning and made another tiny adjustment to her hat. The miserable deaths of a large number of furred and feathered creatures all over the globe had contributed to its production and Mrs Smicksmack was very proud of it. If the animals could have seen the satisfaction it brought to her beautiful, green eyes they would probably have smiled in their corner of heaven, knowing that they had not laid down their lives in vain. Quite convinced that not even Mrs Pottelnuss could be wearing anything to compare with it, Mrs Smicksmack entered the lift and floated earthwards with angelic composure. How envious they would all be at the Ladies' Circle coffee morning! How rare a thing was good taste!

At the street door she met Mrs Klotz and the Poodle.

'Ah, good morning, my dear. Quite a surprise! And I see you have Mr Nebula's marvellous dog with you.'

'Marvellous?' Mrs Klotz clenched her teeth. 'I could tell you some things about this marvellous dog, Mrs

Smicksmack, that would . . . .'

But Mrs Smicksmack was not in a mood to listen. She saw no reason why she should allow her high spirits to be depressed on such a glorious morning. Mrs Klotz could be very dreary sometimes. She raised a perfumed hand.

'Do tell me all about it later, my dear. At the moment I am a little late for an appointment. Do you like my hat?' and she slid onto the leather upholstery of SMICK 500, her large, pink convertible (Mr Smicksmack's car, SMACK 500, was in pearl grey) and waved adieu.

The Iron Poodle kept very close to Mrs Klotz as she stumped up the stairs, so as not to be garrotted by the lead.

The door-chimes played the first few notes of the 'Blue Danube' waltz and Mrs Klotz went to see who was there. She looked hot.

'Butcher's boy, missus. I've brought Mrs Smicksmack's order.'

'Haven't seen you before, have I?' said Mrs Klotz, staring at the unfamiliar face.

'No, missus. Just started today.'

'Hmm. Well, put the meat in the kitchen, Gingernut. It's down that passage and on the right. I'm busy so close the door behind you when you go out.'

'Righto, missus.'

Mrs Klotz went back to heaving the feather bolsters out of the bedroom window to air them.

The Iron Poodle looked up attentively from his refuge under a gilded French chair. Something about the butcher's boy seemed familiar, but he couldn't make out what. The boy stood staring round the room for a moment, without noticing the dog under the chair. Then he picked up a small object from a table and put it into his pocket. The Poodle blinked. Curious, he thought.

A few paces took the boy to the end of the passage, where he appeared to spend some time gazing out of the window. After a while he carried the meat into the kitchen and walked out of the flat whistling.

'No, Mrs Krug, definitely not tonight. Sorry, but I just can't turn my back on him for a minute. You know what he's like.'

Kaspar heard a parched rumbling that must have been Old Krug's reply, then his mother came back alone.

'She'll just have to buy her own tonight, that's all there is to it.'

Mrs Klotz kicked off her slippers and curled up on the settee in one of Smicksmack's favourite poses.

'Turn that row off, Kaspar. I'm trying to do a crossword. Eight across – the fruit of the paw-paw tree, six letters.'

She frowned. Kaspar turned down the volume of his radio and sighed. The programme was an adventure play, not a very good one. The hero had too much luck.

'Paw-paw,' he offered.

'That's what I said – paw-paw tree,' replied Mrs Klotz. The Iron Poodle groaned.

'I mean paw-paw is the answer,' Kaspar said.

She looked up. 'Oh, don't be so ridiculous, Kaspar. They wouldn't make it as obvious as that!'

'Perhaps it's a double bluff?'

'Haven't you got any more homework to do?'

'No.'

'Well then, sit quietly. I hate being helped.'

She wriggled into a more comfortable position and made a first attack on the clue. But the subject of fruit suggested food and her mind kept wandering to the Smicksmacks at the banquet. She could just imagine Mrs Smicksmack getting her teeth into the smoked salmon! She hadn't eaten a mouthful all day to make sure she could gorge herself tonight. She was disgusting at times. Mrs Klotz hoped that her moonstones would fall into the soup.

Kaspar twiddled the dial for a bit, then sank into a stupor. The pages of the *Boys' Own Wonder Book of Useful Things to Know* remained unopened as the Poodle dropped into a fitful doze. Going to bed seemed the most exciting prospect the evening offered.

Half an hour later Mrs Klotz's voice announced with pride, 'I've got it! It's "paw-paw". It must have been a double bluff!'

The window moved up noiselessly as Ferdy pushed at it from the landing of the fire escape. All the lights in the flat were off and the only sound was the brumming of the ice-box in the kitchen. He clambered over the sill and switched his torch on, keeping the beam directed to the floor. 'Come on,' he whispered. 'It's O.K. They won't be back for hours!'

Mr Smicksmack grinned through his discomfort. Ever since he had taken to wearing a wig he had been plagued by the idea that one day his secret would be discovered in public. He watched now with horrified fascination as the bow of the gypsy violinist scraped closer and closer to his right ear. If it came an inch nearer, the wig would be lifted clean off his head and everyone around the huge table would see how bald he was! Suddenly, he could bear it no longer. He tore a handful of notes from his trouser-pocket and shoved them in the gypsy's direction.

'Push off!' he murmured through his cigar.

The gypsy's top lip curled up with the speed of a roller-blind and a reptilian hiss escaped between the gap in his teeth. But his eyes softened when he saw the size of the tip. He grasped it expertly between the upper and lower incisors and loped off to the furthest conglomeration of diners, where he began to serenade an ancient lady, who was obviously propped up by her ear-trumpet and corsets. Mrs Smicksmack went the colour of plum jam. She had been enjoying a little moment of glory, leaning back in her chair and smiling wistfully as the violinist had played only for her. She had just been thinking that leaning backwards made the moonstones sparkle rather nicely, when she found

herself staring at a patch of striped wallpaper where the gypsy had been. It made her feel slightly peculiar. She was aware that people did not smile wistfully at the wallpaper during banquets. She sat up with a gay little laugh and covered her mouth with her hand.

'Why did you do that?' Her tone was icy.

'What?'

'You know very well! Why did you get rid of the gypsy?'

'I was jealous,' he said.

'Oh, really!' said Mrs Smicksmack. 'You flatterer!' But she was convinced that he was lying.

The Astoria Ballroom band struck up a jolly little tune called 'When the Ostrich Eats his Breakfast' and dozens of plump, glittering women began to drag dozens of fat, sleepy husbands onto the dance floor. The bandleader, who fancied an early night, took everything at a fast tempo and succeeded in clearing the floor by half past twelve.

'Not bad,' he remarked to the first trombone as they made for the beer and sandwiches.

Mrs Smicksmack sat outside in SMACK 500 (the pearl grey one) while Mr Smicksmack collected her mink stole. She was sure that this car didn't go well with her new hair colour and she was wondering which it would be less tiresome to change. She yawned and drummed her fingers impatiently on the cocktail cabinet. Was it worthwhile raising the matter of the gypsy violinist again, or should she save it for a future occasion? She would see when they got home.

The indigestion powder fizzed cheerily in the tumbler and Mr Smicksmack was halfway through a much-needed gulp, when a scream came from the dressing room. Something of an urgent nature in the scream persuaded Mr Smicksmack that his wife had not merely stepped on the cat. He finished choking and looked about for a weapon of defence. He seized the long-handled brush that he normally used for scrubbing his back and made his way warily to the source of the noise. A peep around the door showed him nothing out of the ordinary except Mrs Smicksmack banging on the floor with her fists and howling furiously. As he entered (deftly disencumbering himself of the bathbrush) she raised a tear-stained face. 'It's gone!' she sobbed. 'My jewel case! I know exactly where I left it this time and it isn't there any more!'

Mr Smicksmack passed a shaking hand over his forehead. Then he went back to the bathroom to finish the indigestion powder.

Kaspar turned over in bed and woke himself up. No, he hadn't been dreaming. It *was* the sound of a police car!

He leaped out from under the quilt and ran to the window. The Poodle joined him and they looked at the block across the street. Lights from two police cars were flashing regularly across the frontage and everywhere, windows were opening and pyjamaed people were leaning out. Passers-by had stopped and a small crowd was already forming and gazing upward. Kaspar looked again. The only apartment to be fully lit up was the Smicksmacks'! Whatever had caused this disturbance must have taken place there! The figure of a policeman stood framed by the drawing-room curtains. Kaspar hopped out of his own room and banged on his mother's door.

A little later, he was urging her to speed up from the end of her bed.

'Oh, come on, come on! It will all be over before we get there!'

Mrs Klotz did not reply but took out the last curler and brushed her hair vigorously. Then she slipped into her coat and shoes and hurried out with Kaspar. The Iron Poodle followed closely. As they passed Mrs Krug's her door opened and a frightened face showed in the gap. 'What's going on? Are we all going to be murdered?'

Mrs Klotz called over her shoulder, 'Something's up at Smicksmacks'. I'll have to take a look!'

'Well, I never,' grumbled Mrs Krug. 'Still, I'm not surprised.'

Oscar slipped out between her legs and headed downstairs.

'Where are *you* going now? You're supposed to keep me company! Ungrateful little beast.'

She shut the door, sat down, then stood up again. Finally, she decided that she would go and see what was happening for herself.

The crowd outside the Smicksmacks' building was now quite a large one. Mrs Klotz and Kaspar had to battle their way through to get to the front. Here they were stopped by a policeman. 'Are you a relation of the Smicksmacks, madam?'

'No,' replied Mrs Klotz, 'But I work there so if anything's wrong I'm bound to be needed. This is my son,' she added, as the policeman stepped aside. 'And his dog,' she explained, as the Iron Poodle entered in their wake.

'Any more?' the policeman asked, wryly.

''Course not!' said Mrs Klotz, to whom his tone had been indistinguishable from cheek.

They were stopped again at the entrance to the flat and Mrs Klotz was obliged to repeat her explanations. Inside, the place was a stew of detectives, finger-print experts, photographers and newspaper reporters. Seeing a familiar figure, Mrs Smicksmack swept down on Mrs Klotz and sobbed out the dreadful story while hanging about her neck. (This ensured that her own, tragic face was nearest the cameras.) Mrs Klotz was suitably appalled but, after all, it was hardly surprising. She had been warning Mrs Smicksmack for months to find a safer hiding place for the jewel case and she had taken absolutely no notice. She reminded Mrs Smicksmack of this fact gently and was just about to suggest that she make everyone a cup of coffee when she saw Mrs Smicksmack stiffen and a very strange expression came over her face. Kaspar looked at them both, wondering what had happened and one of the detectives approached.

'But Mrs Klotz,' Mrs Smicksmack was saying, 'I've

just remembered! I *did* take the advice you gave me the other day. I *did* hide the jewel case behind the dressing-room ventilator. And nobody could have known about it but us!'

'Are you absolutely certain of what you just said?' interrupted the detective.

'Positive!' said Mrs Smicksmack.

'I see. In that case, Mrs Klotz, would you come over here for a moment? There are one or two questions I should like to ask you.'

Kaspar grabbed hold of his mother about the waist. Her face had gone the colour of vanilla blancmange. Someone else would have to make the coffee.

10

'I know, dear, I know. Yes, don't I just know it!'

Mrs Krug laid a comforting arm on Mrs Klotz's shoulder.

'You don't have to tell me anything about rich folks. Didn't I work for Mrs Zubnik for nigh on fifteen years and she still had to count all the sugar lumps every time I came back with the groceries! They trust no one, Mrs Klotz dear, and they're the first to accuse you if anything goes wrong.'

Mrs Klotz buried her nose (which was extra red from much weeping) in her coffee cup and swallowed deeply.

'That's right, dear. You drink your coffee and try to forget about it.'

'Forget about it!' Mrs Klotz exclaimed. 'Forget about it! I'll never forget this as long as I breathe! Not till my name is cleared! Do you know, Mrs Krug, that even Mr G . . . .' A wave of emotion rendered her speechless.

'Who, dear?'

'Even Mr G . . . rinser,' she resumed, 'cold-shouldered me when I told him what had happened.'

'No, Mrs Klotz!'

'Yes, indeed, Mrs Krug. Said it wasn't any of his business and that the police would sort it all out and would I excuse him because he had to get his meat orders ready.'

'No – after the way he's behaved towards you! It just goes to show, Mrs Klotz. When a woman's on her own, she's on her own. That's all there is to it.'

Kaspar had taken as much of all this as he could stand. Old Krug was a blight at any time of the day, but when she weighed-in at breakfast, life was becoming intolerable. Besides, he had urgent things to do. He scraped the remains of the scrambled egg into his mouth, snatched his schoolbag and strode to the door. Here he paused and turned to look at the miserable figure of his mother. 'Don't worry,' he said. 'It'll be all right.' He would have said more, possibly, but the presence of Krug put him off.

'Wouldn't you like Kaspar to stay with you today, Mrs Klotz? Missing school wouldn't matter for once and you might find him a comfort.' (She didn't sound very convinced.)

He dashed out. *His* plans for the day were different and they didn't include staying in with his mother *or* going to school. The schoolbag was just an alibi.

The Poodle bounded behind him as he ran along the path and when he left the garden he was in such a hurry that he forgot to give the gate its usual bang. He grabbed the waiting Matty by the satchel straps and pulled him along the Schiller Avenue.

'Hey, what's the big idea?' gasped Matty. 'Are you specially keen to give Pelikan his good-morning kiss, or is your mother after you with a knife?'

'Idiot!' fumed Kaspar. 'There's no time to explain now, but we're not going to school this morning. We're going to pick up Johnnie and Christa and then we're heading for Nebula's apartment. I've got something really important to tell you all. And then we've got to act fast!'

A little out of breath they clustered around Kaspar in the small, panelled room where the Poodle had first shown them the chest.

'All right, tell!' said Johnnie, who was wondering nervously what would happen when they didn't show up to answer the register.

'Here goes,' said Kaspar. And he outlined all the events of the previous night.

Johnnie gave a low whistle. 'Smicksmack's jewels? They must be worth a fortune! She must be mad to get them back!'

'So is my mother,' Kaspar added. 'In fact, she'd be so glad that I bet we'd have no further trouble about the Poodle.'

Christa's eyes widened. 'You mean you think she'd let us keep him if we recovered the jewels for Mrs Smicksmack?'

'I'm sure of it. Just think of the favour she would owe us.'

'There's only one thing wrong with all this,' interjected Johnnie, gloomily. 'We haven't got the faintest idea where to look for the jewel case. And we know no more than the police about who actually stole it.'

'Is that so?' said Kaspar tensely. 'Well, I've had a long time to think about this and I'll give you three guesses who I think it is!'

Johnnie frowned for a second. Then a thought struck him. 'You don't mean . . . ?'

'Well?'

'But they wouldn't dare! They're not much older than us! How would they get rid of stuff like that?'

'One moment,' said the Poodle, who was getting quite confused by now. 'You haven't said who you think the culprits *are* yet.'

Johnnie glanced at him. 'It's Kaspar's theory, not mine. He seems to think the guilty ones are Rudolph and his gang.'

'Hmm,' replied the Poodle, thoughtfully. 'I wonder if I can shed a little light on the matter.'

'What do you know about this?' asked Kaspar.

'Well it may or may not have anything to do with it, but when I was at the Smicksmacks' apartment yesterday . . . .' And he told them about the butcher's boy and his curious behaviour.

'Your mother referred to him as "Gingernut" on account of his carroty hair.'

'A redhead!' declared Matty. 'That could only have been Ferdy!'

'What did I tell you?' said Kaspar. 'I knew it must be them! But what made him choose to dress up as one of Grinser's boys?'

A strange light began to dawn in his eyes. 'We've got to find out where they are!'

'Yes,' said Christa, 'and *soon* – before they get a chance to get rid of that loot!'

Mr Grinser unbolted the side door leading into the back shop cautiously and opened it just wide enough to admit his guest. The portly figure in a heavy, dark coat had turned up his fur collar and pulled down his broad brimmed hat the better to conceal his face. He paused for a moment and took in the scene. Rudolph, Ferdy and Ernst were lounging round one of the scrubbed chopping-blocks that acted as a makeshift table and the open jewel case lay in the centre on a remnant of blue-checked cloth.

'I've got to open up in half an hour,' said Grinser, nervously. 'We'd better make it quick.'

'Suits me,' said the fat man in the overcoat. He fitted a jeweller's eyeglass in position. 'O.K., let's see what you've got.'

'They could be anywhere!' moaned Johnnie. 'There must be over a thousand streets in Koningshaven, and if every street has a hundred houses and some of them are divided into flats, then they could be hiding in a million different places! What chance have we got of finding them? Wouldn't it be better if we just went and told the police? They've got all sorts of methods for tracing criminals.'

'No,' Kaspar said firmly. 'We're going to do this ourselves. And when we catch them, *we'll* take all the credit.'

'But how?' persisted Johnnie. 'We sit here talking and they could be making a getaway at this very minute!'

The Poodle roused himself and stretched (they had been sitting down for some time). 'There's only one thing to be done,' he said impressively.

'What's that?' asked Kaspar.

'Follow me,' said the Poodle. 'It doesn't always work – in fact you can usually rely on it to break down just when you need it – but the only thing that might get us a quick result is Mr Nebula's crystal ball.'

Some very peculiar expressions were visible after this statement, but as no one actually *said* anything, Kaspar merely shrugged his shoulders and they all got to their feet.

They trooped out of the panelled chamber and followed the Poodle down the passage. At the end was a cast iron staircase they'd never noticed before. It seemed to go up to the roof. The Poodle ascended energetically and they clonked up behind him.

'Be careful,' he warned. 'The treads are slippery!' They emerged in the corner of an extensive attic painted black, but lit by a huge skylight in the middle of the ceiling. Below it, on a stand about three feet from the floor, was a large, crystal globe that caught and concentrated all the available light. Rainbow patches flickered on the black walls and played on specks of dust as they rose and sank.

'I'll just crank it up,' said the Poodle, and he gave a turn to a handle on the column. 'Now, sit down around it and try to concentrate on what you want to see. If we are exceptionally fortunate it may work first time.'

The ball went into a rapid spin. At first, it flashed so

brightly that they were dazzled and had to squint at it. Then the interior of the crystal went dark and they only saw little pinpricks of light, like stars. A milky-white sphere appeared, revolving slowly in space.

'That's the Earth,' whispered Christa.

'Good,' said the Poodle. 'Then we would seem to be roughly in the right place.'

Johnnie snorted. 'It'll have to do better than that!'

'Give it time,' sighed the Poodle. 'It's only just getting warmed up. And it is rather an *old* crystal ball.'

Suddenly, they saw a tropical forest. The colours were brilliant. A monkey sitting in the fork of a tree was chewing a banana and spitting bits out. One of these bits landed in the water-pot an old woman was carrying by on her head. Then the picture changed. Miss Poltergeist's face swam into view. A class of boys was sitting in her form room with their heads down over their books. When no one was looking, Miss Poltergeist removed a large chocolate from her pencil case and pushed it quickly into her mouth. Guiltily, she devoured it with rapid sucks.

'Someone's thinking about *food*!' roared Kaspar.

'Not me!' said Matty quickly.

'Or me!'

'Or me!'

'And certainly not *I*!' the Poodle said haughtily. 'Anyway, we're getting nearer.'

'Look. What's this?'

The stars had re-appeared, but somehow they looked different. They were much larger and much closer together.

Kaspar shrugged. Then his eyes widened. 'They're not stars at all! They're diamonds!'

'And rubies,' breathed Christa, as fresh stones were revealed.

'And sapphires! And an emerald!' added Johnnie.

Matty just gaped.

'Got them at last,' said the Poodle. 'Now if only the crystal would scan round a bit we could see whereabouts they are.'

But at that instant, Miss Poltergeist's huge face returned, still working on the chocolate.

'Drat the thing,' snapped the Poodle. 'It's always doing this.'

He sprang forward and gave it a bang. And that did the trick. All at once they found themselves looking at five figures crouching around a curious table. One of them was holding a gemstone up to the light and examining it through an eyeglass. The scene of the activity was unmistakable. They were in Mr Grinser's back shop! There was Mr Grinser himself, looking drawn and anxious under his straw boater, and there were Rudolph, Ferdy and Ernst, looking greedily at the stones.

'That's it!' yelled Kaspar. 'That's where we'll find them! Come on. Let's get there straight away!' But the words were no sooner spoken when the crystal ball shimmered eerily and they saw themselves reflected in it. They also saw the reflection of someone else standing in the same room. Their triumph evaporated. One by

one they turned around slowly, hardly daring to look in case it was real. It was real, all right. There, in the corner by the staircase, stood Mr Nebula.

The Poodle gulped and began to grope for an excuse, but Mr Nebula raised a hand impatiently. 'I have seen and understood everything.'

'What are you going to do with us?' asked Kaspar, realising that this was a time for tact.

'Do with you?' said Mr Nebula grimly. 'The answer to your question is obvious, young man.' He took a step towards them. 'I am going to help you!'

'Help us? Oh, well done, Mr Nebula!'

Their excitement burst out like a champagne cork. They clattered across the wooden floor and jumped up and down around him till they were dizzy. Only Kaspar stood apart, waiting to see what would happen next.

Mr Nebula put a hand to his brow. 'All right. Be quiet. Keep still for a moment. The cat is not in the bag yet! Now,' he continued, when the atmosphere was calmer, 'you must get to the butcher's shop immediately. Make sure that you post a guard on both entrances - and see that no one leaves the building until the police appear. Then they will see that you are the ones who are responsible for the capture of the thieves.'

'What about you, Mr Nebula? Aren't you coming with us?'

'I shall come after you as soon as possible, Kaspar. But first, I have some telephoning to do. Now, go on, all of you. Let's pray we are not too late.'

The Iron Poodle was last to go down the spiral staircase. As he passed him by, Mr Nebula wagged a finger at him reprovingly and made a bad-tempered clicking with his tongue. But the Poodle was glad to note that his eyes did not look angry.

Ten minutes later they stood panting in the little alleyway at the side of Grinser's shop. 'Take this,' ordered Kaspar, undoing the Poodle's lead. 'You know how to stop them if they try coming out at the front.'

Johnnie and Christa crept round into the Avenue.

'Keep well down out of sight!' he whispered after them.

Two or three delivery bicycles leant against the wall by the side door. With Kaspar's help, Matty clambered up onto one to get a view through a high, square window. It looked directly into the back shop. Cautiously he raised his eyes and about half of his nose just above the sill. Then he dropped back noiselessly into the lane.

'Still there?'

'Yes,' panted Matty. 'The man with the eyeglass was taking out a wad of notes. They can't be planning to stay much longer.'

'Help me, then,' said Kaspar. 'We'd better put the bikes in front of this door.'

Mr Nebula replaced the receiver and picked up a heavy walking stick. It might come in useful, he thought. The police were on their way to Grinser's and Mr and Mrs Smicksmack were bringing Mrs Klotz. As he left his apartment he remembered that he was still wearing his indoor smoking cap. There was no time to change it so he shoved it into his pocket. Then it occurred to him that he was always rather odd-looking anyway. He took it out and put it back on his head.

'A pleasure to do business with you, Mr Grinser.' The fat man stood up and shook hands all round. 'And with you gentlemen, of course. You'll bear me in mind, I hope, if ever you have any more little items to dispose of?'

They looked at the pile of notes on the table and nodded.

'You know where to get in touch with me if you need me.'

He walked to the door and Grinser slid back the bolt. 'I'll just check there's no one about before you go.'

Grinser opened the door and peeped out. What he saw caused his jaw to drop and his eyelids to peel back horrifically. Three bicycles had been erected to form a barricade across the entrance and there, behind them, stood Kaspar Klotz and another boy, brandishing the pumps. Kaspar's poodle had bared its teeth.

'What are you playing at, Kaspar, you little maggot?' growled Grinser. 'Get those bikes out of the way at once!'

At that precise moment a police siren began to wail in the distance.

'Here, what's going on?' said the fat man. He pushed Grinser to one side and got a stomach-full of bicycle. The police siren sounded in his ears.

'Police!' he shouted. 'Let me get out of here!' and he heaved a fat leg over the tangle of bikes.

'Me too!' shrieked Grinser. Terrified at being caught with the evidence, he threw himself on the fat man's back.

'Get off!' he spluttered. 'We can't both get out at once.'

Grinser's nerve snapped. 'Me first! Me first!'

They rocked and swayed on the heap of machinery and the jewel case slipped from the fat man's pocket.

'Look out!' he screamed. 'Let me through, you idiot!' as the pair crashed down at Kaspar's feet.

Ernst and Ferdy were not slow in getting the message. They snatched up the cash that lay on the table and beat a retreat through the front shop. There they opened the door and dashed out, not noticing the dog lead that was stretched across their path. Ferdy hit the pavement, then Ernst hit Ferdy and the banknotes rained on them like confetti. The first police car appeared at the corner of the street.

'Why, you little . . . ' gasped Grinser, struggling to his feet.'

Kaspar stepped back and raised the bicycle pump. The fat man scrabbled across the alley and tried to get at the jewel case. But he didn't make it. Rudolf, who had been waiting for his chance, leapt lightly onto one of the bicycles, swept up the case and stuffed it into his shirt. He turned to bolt for the Schiller Avenue but the police car swerved in and blocked his exit. SMACK 500 (in pearl grey) swung in behind it. He wheeled about and pedalled furiously in the opposite direction.

'Stop him!' shouted Kaspar, banging Grinser on the head. 'Stop him, someone, he's got the jewels!'

The Iron Poodle bounded forward and followed Rudolf up the lane. He put on a burst of speed just as Rudolf braked to take the turn and jumped into the rear wicker basket used to deliver meat. Rudolf wobbled and almost came off but he recovered skilfully and began to accelerate. The Poodle answered with an ear-splitting series of howls and barks.

'Come on, Matty!' said Kaspar (giving Grinser another bang for luck). 'The police can handle these two. Let's take the other bikes and get after Rudolf!'

Four policemen puffed up and shoved Grinser and the fat man into the car. A second police vehicle arrived.

'Quick!' said one of the first policemen. 'One of them's got away on a delivery bike. You can't miss it. There's a poodle in the back!'

The second car reversed out and tore off round the block with SMACK 500 in hot pursuit. Mr Smicksmack (who rarely drove) stepped on the accelerator too enthusiastically and the screams of Mrs Smicksmack, Mrs Klotz and Mrs Krug were terrible to hear as they sped down the Schiller Avenue.

Now began the chase that took them halfway over Koningshaven. Rudolf was in front, pedalling for dear life, with the Iron Poodle yowling fit to burst in the basket. Just behind, on their lighter mounts, Kaspar and Matty were gradually cutting his lead by inches. And bringing up the rear were SMACK 500 and the police cars, windows wide to follow the Poodle's signal.

Traffic screeched to a halt and pedestrians scattered in every direction as the cavalcade rushed by. Rudolf knew the area like the back of his hand and chose the most unlikely streets to throw off his pursuers. He changed course and doubled back at every opportunity. But every time he looked behind he saw Kaspar and Matty making up ground and heard, like a gathering hornet swarm, the sound of more police sirens. His energy couldn't last for ever. Police cars were converging on the area from every corner of the city. His one chance was to get indoors - a pub, a café, a cinema - anywhere that would get him off the dangerous streets! At last he tried a desperate measure. He cut across a busy square and headed down the Groat Market, a narrow street choked with crowds of shoppers and traders' stalls. If he could make it to the other end he would reach a spot where three ways met. That would give him a final chance to dump the Poodle and give them all the slip! He plunged into the mass of bodies and zig-zagged over the cobbles.

Kaspar and Matty whizzed over the square after him and braked at the entrance to the market. Their hearts sank when they saw the route that he had taken and they jumped off their bikes to try to push a way through. The Poodle's barks were growing fainter and fainter and they knew that they were losing precious time. Old boxes and piles of rubbish slowed them down further and the cobblestones were slippery with rotten fruit. Suddenly, they had a clear view of Rudolf near the bottom of the alley. He had kept up a high speed and seemed all set to leave them behind for good. Their lungs were bursting. 'Oh no!' groaned Kaspar. 'He's going to make it. Come on, Matty. Run!'

Then they saw an old man pushing a barrow load of oranges round the corner into the street. Kaspar stopped and grabbed Matty's arm. They watched, panting. Rudolf tried to avoid the approaching orange-man, who could not see him over the enormous pyramid of fruit, but he was going too fast and there was no room to manoeuvre. There was an explosive *crack*! and a thousand blood-red oranges erupted and fell in a shower. All at once, the Iron Poodle stopped barking.

Police sirens screamed behind them. Tyres scraped against the kerb. Kaspar and Matty clawed their way through the crowd to see what had happened to Rudolf. He was lying unconscious near the pavement, half smothered by oranges, and the Iron Poodle sat on his chest with the jewel case in his mouth. Car doors slammed and the police rushed past them. Mrs Klotz screeched and hurled herself on Kaspar. Mrs Smicksmack gave a bigger screech and threw herself on the jewel case. Mrs Krug, though she hadn't much to screech about, didn't want to feel left out of things so she flung herself round the neck of Mr Nebula (who had appeared mysteriously out of nowhere) and sobbed even louder than the others. Rudolf, chalky-faced and limp, was carried off to meet his fate.

Mrs Klotz put two teaspoonfuls of sugar into her coffee and stirred it vigorously.

'No. Definitely not. I wouldn't go back to work for Mrs Smicksmack if she paid me ten times as much. It's the principle of the thing, Mrs Krug.'

Old Krug sighed. 'Well, I suppose you know your own mind. Meat'll be pricy again, with that crook Grinser in prison. I don't see how you'll manage, dear, really I don't.'

'Don't worry about us, Mrs Krug, we'll survive.'

She walked out into the passage where Kaspar and the Poodle were ready to leave. The Iron Poodle looked cheerful enough, but Kaspar was sullen. 'Hope it keeps fine for you,' she said. 'It looked like rain earlier.'

They pattered down the stairs together and out into the dark night,

'Remember,' her voice called after them. 'Be back here before half past twelve. And I want *exactly* fifty per cent!'

Other Titles in Andersen Young Readers' Library

Carol Adorjan	*The Cat Sitter Mystery*
Roy Brown	*The Big Test* *Chips and the Black Moth* *Chips and the River Rat* *A Nag Called Wednesday*
Frank Charles	*Beyond the Midnight Mountains*
Philip Curtis	*Mr Browser and the Comet Crisis* *Mr Browser Meets the Burrowers* *The Revenge of the Brain Sharpeners*
Elfie Donnelly	*Odd Stockings* *So Long, Grandpa*
Peter Hartling	*Theo Runs Away*
Geoffrey Hayes	*Patrick Comes to Puttyville*
Hans-Eric Hellberg	*The One-Eyed Bandits*
Christine Nostlinger	*Conrad* *Lollipop*
Jan Procházka	*The Carp*
Nora Rock	*Monkey's Perfect* *Rope Around the Wind*

Joyce Rockwood	*Groundhog's Horse*
Margaret Rogers	*Cindy and the Silver Enchantress* *The Time Stone*
Brenda Sivers	*Biminy in Danger*
Angela Sommer-Bodenburg	*The Little Vampire* *The Little Vampire Moves In*
Hazel Townson	*The Great Ice-Cream Crime* *The Speckled Panic*
Ursula Moray Williams	*Jeffy, the Burglar's Cat*
Ursula Wölfel	*Shooting Star*
M. A. Wood	*Master Deor's Apprentice*